CW00871964

Driftwood

From the Shannon to the Marne

Harry Sheehy

Order this book online at www.trafford.com/08-1578
or email orders@trafford.com

Most Trafford titles are also available at major online book retailers.

Note for Librarians: A cataloguing record for this book is available from Library
and Archives Canada at www.collectionscanada.ca/amicus/index-e.html

ISBN: 978-1-4269-0056-3 (soft)
ISBN: 978-1-4269-0058-7 (ebook)

*We at Trafford believe that it is the responsibility of us all, as both individuals
and corporations, to make choices that are environmentally and socially sound.
You, in turn, are supporting this responsible conduct each time you purchase a
Trafford book, or make use of our publishing services. To find out how you are
helping, please visit www.trafford.com/responsiblepublishing.html*

*Our mission is to efficiently provide the world's finest, most comprehensive
book publishing service, enabling every author to experience success.
To find out how to publish your book, your way, and have it available
worldwide, visit us online at www.trafford.com/10510*

 www.trafford.com

North America & international
toll-free: 1 888 232 4444 (USA & Canada)
phone: 250 383 6864 ♦ fax: 250 383 6804 ♦ email: info@trafford.com

The United Kingdom & Europe
phone: +44 (0)1865 487 395 ♦ local rate: 0845 230 9601
facsimile: +44 (0)1865 481 507 ♦ email: info.uk@trafford.com

To Marion

Harry Sheehy was born in Dublin in 1963 to Gerard & Agnes Sheehy. He left school at the age of fifteen, much to the relief of the school staff and his fellow pupils. He trained as a chef for two years and eventually became Ireland's worst-ever chef. Accepting failure is one of his greatest strengths. In 1981 he joined the Irish army where he kept a low profile for the next twenty-seven years. He served in Lebanon, Israel, and Iraq. He returned to school at the age of thirty-eight and sat his Leaving Certificate just before his fortieth birthday. This time around he was a little less disruptive in class. He later trained as a software engineer in Dundalk Institute of Technology and moved to the Signals Corps. He retired from the army in 2008 without anyone noticing.

He is married to Marion and they have two boys, both of whom consider him a constant source of embarrassment to the family.

He has had an unnatural relationship with the inland waterways since childhood. He has owned several small boats but his favourite one was an old wooden former ship's lifeboat that used to sink on him with alarming regularity.

Acknowledgments

It's a sad fact that in the nature of book writing it is assumed that the book is written by one person. There may be only one author, but there are a great many other people involved too. I am probably the worst speller on this planet, and I owe a huge debt of gratitude to the following who gave of their free time to sit down with a red pen, and reams of A4, and correct spelling, grammar, and the many silly typos, as well as offering good advice:

Gerard Sheehy, Bunny Firth, Aidan Sheehy, Ann Sheehy, Geraldine Warner, and David Duffy. If you do find an error, go and see them.

Thanks to all those who crewed along the way, to Tony O'Connor, Ben Sheehy, Malachy Quinn, Aidan Sheehy, Ann Sheehy, Barry Humphreys. Most of all I want to thank my Dad, and first mate, Gerard Sheehy, who was with me all the way from Kilrush on the Shannon to Ouistreham in France.

I also want to thank the men and women of the RNLI. When no one else can help, these guys can. I have been a shore-based member for many years, and ten percent of my royalties from this book is promised to them.

Contents

1. What comes out drunk…went in sober   1

1. The Atlantic beckons and the fools rush in   22

1. Beginners' Luck   34

1. Our Nemesis The Celtic Sea   53

1. The problem with reptiles.   68

1. Ooh la la, it's the Channel   91

1. Three wheels on my wagon   104

1. On our last leg   111

1. Legless   120

1. Vive La Difference   137

Foreword

I have wanted to go on this trip to France for a great many years. At night I would lie in bed and dream of the challenges that it would pose: the swells, and the waves, the mechanical problems, the seasickness, the navigation problems, and the tides.

I planned everything down to the last detail. In the evenings I would turn on Google Earth and scan every inch of the planned route. I measured distances, did calculations, then measured the distances again to make sure that they were correct. I read every book I could get my hands on in an attempt to satisfy my desire to venture into new environs. But instead of satisfying my desire, I fed my ambition. Slowly I planned every facet of the route. I prepared the boat and did a navigation course.

In the military they say that 'No plan survives the battle.' Plans must be able to adapt and that is what we had to do. We didn't stick to the planned route, and for good reasons too. We changed things as we learned more, and we learned a lot, and we learned more every day.

I had been cruising the Irish inland waterways since childhood and I was getting itchy feet. I wanted to go along a waterway where I didn't know what was around the next bend. But it was more than that. If that was all it was I could have just put my boat *Driftwood* on a truck and shipped it to France. I wanted an adventure, to take a few chances and see if it would come out alright in the end, and, thankfully, it did.

I have written this book so that I can share this experience with as many people as possible. I want you to feel as though you are a member of the crew, and not an envious bystander. I want you to be a part of it.

So please come and join me, step on board *Driftwood* and let's go on an adventure.

Chapter One

What comes out drunk...went in sober

I TURNED IN THE bed again. I couldn't sleep, I couldn't get comfortable. Sometimes I felt sleep sneaking up on me but then it bolted away as soon as I was aware of its presence. It's easy to become annoyed with yourself when you can't sleep. I decided to count sheep. It didn't work; there were only thirty-five of them. We had gone to bed early and I really just wasn't that tired. Marion on the other hand was. "Come on and get up Mar and we will go for a walk." It was just after 11pm and Marion, who had no difficulty sleeping, reluctantly got up after a bit more coaxing and we carefully stepped off the boat onto the floating jetty. The crisp air contrasted with the warmth of the bed. The stars shone through a black backdrop as we walked the jetty.

Before too long we came across Tommy and Marge on their boat *Free Spirit*. "Hi guys, come on in for a beer. Ah sure ye couldn't say no, that'd be rude." We had a beer and then a few more beers. We discussed the usual things that you discuss when you're full to spilling point - global warming, trouble in the Gulf. I vaguely remember a bit about world peace and then I told Tommy that I planned to sail my boat to France. You tell people things when you're pissed that you really should keep to yourself. Tommy's advice, though interesting and well intentioned, if not very helpful, was to "Strap a dirty big outboard engine to the back of yer boat, just in case you break down, it will give you a way to get ashore safely." At the time we did give it serious thought. We drank more beer and did more planning, and so that's how my plan became public knowledge and the joke of the River Shannon. Tommy doesn't do discreet.

There were a few problems I needed to overcome if I intended taking my boat on a serious sea voyage. There were a few more problems when you consider that I had little, or close to no, sea experience. Neither had my Dad, whom I hoped would crew with me. And if that wasn't bad enough, Driftwood although a fine boat, is only thirty-three feet long, she is twenty-four years old, and she is a river/estuary cruiser, not a sea boat.

So I decided that it would be a good idea to first of all bring *Driftwood* down the river as far as Limerick City. Here the Shannon enters the sea, and there is a fifty-mile-long estuary. This is where I planned to see how she handled the swells, to see if she had enough power to take on the ocean and to find out if I was prone to seasickness. It may seem silly but seasickness is enough to prevent you from doing any proper navigation, as well as making you a very smelly and unpopular crew member.

Driftwood has two engines, which is a big advantage. However, she is not a fast boat and cruises at about seven to eight knots. That's about the speed someone might jog at. She has an old radar which is mounted on a small radar mast on the front deck. In anticipation of the adventure I fitted an electronic chart plotter. This is a gizmo with a small screen, about the size of a pack of cigarettes that shows your position with a portion of the chart in the background.

So my plan was to do a 'Dry run' if you like, around the estuary, except it would, of course be a wet run. If that went well then I needed to get trained up, and get the boat properly seaworthy, and find a crew.

My insurance only covered me for fresh water. So I needed to arrange cover to potter about in the estuary.

When you ring boat insurance companies they have already decided to treat you as inept even before they answer the phone to you. They try to redirect you to a call-answering centre in Outer Mongolia by using those computerised, "Press one if you have a white boat, or two if you would like to hear Barry Manilow sing *Can't Smile Without You*." I brass-necked it for a full ten minutes and eventually they flinched and then a human came on the phone. He listened to my request to extend my cover to allow me to bring our cruiser down river to the Shannon Estuary: "The tide can run at seven knots on a spring tide you know, and people get swept out into the Atlantic and are never seen again. Do you know what 'wind against tide' is like?" He never mentioned the sea serpents or dragons.

When insurance companies want to stitch you for a really big loading on your policy they say things like "I will have to discuss this with the people upstairs" or "I have to bring it up with the loss assessors" or "I will need to contact the underwriters." The human spoke to all three of them and then looked for €150 for three days' cover.

I have read three books about sea navigation but none of them say what side of the sea you drive on. I don't want to ask so I'll just try to follow someone else. It's important to blend in, you know. I got a tattoo as well.

Mariners have a different word for everything; it's really a different language. This is so that they can tell from your first sentence whether or not you have a clue about maritime matters. To counteract this you find yourself trying to say something nautical so that you can appear knowledgeable on matters of a seafaring nature. But then they catch you out by mentioning fathoms, cardinal markers or their favourite, a dead reckoning. Most mariners can squeeze dead reckonings into the briefest conversations with ease. This is considered a home run.

I told the man in the insurance company that I had a VHF radio but it didn't impress him much. I mentioned the flare pack that I had purchased from a boat chandlers on the advice of someone with a beard and an Aran sweater, and he said he could only reduce the premium if I had completed a Yacht Masters Course with the Royal Yachting Association. This raised the bar on naval qualifications to an unacceptable high. I promised to send off a cheque and hung up quickly before he had a chance to mention dead reckonings. I didn't bother saying anything about the tattoo.

I did my VHF radio course to be legal and compliant. It was two days long and I learned not to say "over and out." Only people, who gained their radio voice procedure experience from watching episodes of Starsky and Hutch, say "Over and out." Nothing betrays a novice over the airwaves quicker.

Eight months later I received my VHF licence. The people who work in the Dept of the Marine are probably very methodical.

Now my VHF is connected to a GPS so that if I ever have to send a Mayday they have a much better chance of finding a body. It should help to bring Marion a certain amount of closure.

I was apprehensive about going out into the estuary. I wanted to see what it is like at sea because *Driftwood* is not really a sea-going boat, it's more a river boat, and shouldn't really be out of its depth, and also because I didn't know just how much it would rock when it met some real waves. Another reason is because I had never been to sea before. Well, I was out in a rib when I used to do scuba diving, and when I was seven years old I got a go in a twelve-foot sailing dingy. I still regret that I ran that aground after only five minutes. It was a humiliating moment, even at seven years of age.

I was determined that if *Driftwood's* sea trials went well we would be sailing to France the following spring. It's a simple plan for a simple man. What could go wrong?

It proved a long trip from our berth in Albert Marina near Drumsna on the northern end of the river Shannon to Limerick at the southern end.

We had decided to use our annual holidays to visit the estuary. We slipped silently along the canal, that is Albert Marina, saying goodbye to friends along the way. Where the canal meets the river a family of swans were rearing their young. I said goodbye to the swans too, but they ignored me. Swans can be very ignorant.

There aren't too many locks on the Shannon and it normally takes about fifteen minutes to go through each one. Rooskey lock is different. In Rooskey lock you can expect to spend about an hour talking to the lock keeper. Tony is a very pleasant guy and very chatty too. This time Mar wanted to get through the lock quickly in order to get across Lough Ree before the wind which was forecast arrived along and messed up our holiday. The trouble is that Tony does nothing in a hurry. He is like a boat and all boats have what they call a hull speed. A hull speed means that no matter how big an engine you put in the boat it can never exceed a speed dictated by the shape of its hull. Tony's hull speed is barge-like.

Mar explained our plight and Tony agreed to lock us through in ten minutes. But he promised to keep us for two hours on the return journey to compensate. True to his word, ten minutes later we were through the lock and on our way again.

At a little after eight in the evening we entered Lough Ree with the sun on our backs and the big lake mirroring the islands and shoreline. A little less than two hours later we sailed into Hodson Bay. A small pillar on an even smaller island in the bay marks the geographical centre of Ireland. Across the lake another island claims the same distinction. It's a bit like "The Oldest Pub in Ireland." Every town has one.

The following morning the wind that was promised arrived, but not as strong as expected. We headed off to Athlone, passing under the By-pass bridge which is lower than you would think. Luckily, I managed to drop the radar mast before the bridge dropped it for me. Athlone is a busy town and I was looking for somewhere quieter, so we passed under the railway bridge and, as luck would have it, a train went overhead at the same moment. As I pondered the stress levels that this old bridge can cope with, another thought occurred to me. What about those "Please don't flush toilets while the train is in the station" notices? What if someone flushed the toilet right then? We passed out the other side of the bridge before the mental image I had formed could materialise.

We passed on through the town and into the lock, which was ready for us. We passed Sean's Bar, a famous watering hole on our right. I have enjoyed many a good pint within its walls over the years. Above the door a sign reads "Ireland's Oldest Pub." The difference is that Sean's pub is actually in the Guinness Book of Records, as the oldest pub in Ireland, so that is fairly definitive.

It had been a while since I was in Athlone lock and I was pleasantly surprised to see that the lock keeper looked twenty-five years younger, had sprouted a full head of hair, grown at least two inches taller, lost about three stone, and had a sex change. The curvy lock keeper locked us through and we continued south.

The wind had grown in strength and it started to rain when we tied up at Clonmacnois. This is one of Ireland's oldest monastic sites. Tour buses, packed with Yanks wearing check trousers, baseball caps, and carrying Nikon cameras with gaudy long lenses, packed the car park. The tourists queued up in line to get ripped off. We joined at the back of the queue. We were shown a short film about Clonmacnois and its long history and then had an even longer walk around the ruins. One thing is for sure: an awful lot of people died in this place at the hands of many raiders, some home-grown, and others from further afield.

We tied up in Shannon Bridge on a nice floating jetty. It had water taps, lighting, and state-of-the-art electric hook-up points, but no electricity. I didn't try the taps but some of the lights surely worked. The sun came out and we sat back and enjoyed the scenery.

A large group of sailors from Athlone Yacht Club were sailing Shannon One class sailing dinghies from Athlone south to Portumna. Unfortunately they had the wind against them and by the time they got to Shannon Bridge they had had enough of it and decided to go to the pub instead. As they approached the bridge they dropped their masts and one by one they tied up and headed for a high stool. One lad thought that he could get under the bridge without dropping his mast. He couldn't, and I think it will be a while before he will forget the embarrassment of wedging his dingy sideways under the bridge in front of all his club mates.

Next morning we headed off to Shannon Harbour, a spot where the Grand Canal from Dublin meets the River Shannon. It's a place of special interest to us both, as in times past we used to keep our boat on this canal close to Dublin. It's a canal we have travelled many times before. After making the long journey from Dublin or Kildare, Shannon Harbour was always a welcome sight. Stepping out from the canal into the river meant an end to the manual locks, horseflies, and also to weed either blocking the water intake for the engine or fouling the propeller.

We tied up, rafting three boats out from the jetty which has a big sign saying *"No Mooring"*. We walked along the towpath to the harbour. The sun was out and the place was full of boats of all kinds, including some that weren't even boats at all. How they were still afloat I just don't know. You could see that this was a place where the normal laws of physics had been suspended. The horseflies remembered me from my last visit and word was spreading quickly. By the time we got back to the boat they had formed an airborne battalion and were doing sorties on me. An F16 fighter pilot wouldn't be able to match their skill. I did manage to inflict a few kills but they left me covered in itchy lumps. We got back on to the Shannon and the horseflies returned to the canal where the food supply is easier to obtain.

We pressed on to Banagher where there is a pub called J.J.Hough's. It's one of the few pubs in Ireland where you can still enjoy a traditional session. It's distinctive on the main street because it is the only pub hidden behind a bush; the bush overgrows the footpath and extends onto the road. Once you have climbed through the undergrowth you find yourself in a superb bar. Some say that it lost some of its character when they modernised it in 1782, but I don't agree. The seats and windowsills have cushions on them that look like they have been there a while, but it all adds to the atmosphere.

A bus trip from Dublin had deposited a gaggle of women into the bar and they excitedly grab seats. "Hey Rose…what's this?" Said one of the women holding up a relatively elderly cushion, "I think it's an incontinence pad!" exclaimed Rose to rapturous laughter from her buddies.

The women took their drinks and settled in. I was sure we could look forward to a few verses of 'Cockles and Mussels' later in the evening

In most joke shops you can buy a green flat cap with a big bush of red hair all around it. People buy them on the rare occasions when the Irish soccer team plays abroad. In Hough's there was a guy wearing the original prototype, only the hair was real, and the Guinness was good too.

An elderly man in a waistcoat covered with lots of badges was sitting in a corner. Suddenly and without any warning he made a couple of short yelping noises and jumped up and down in his seat. A woman made a short screeching noise with a squeeze box and a piano started up and then the man with the badges started beating his leg with the spoons. A bodhrán joined in too. This is what Irish music is all about. As people hid their children under seats or behind curtains we settled into a good session. Everyone had a great night.

The following morning the parents returned and collected the kids they had forgotten from under the seats.

The weather was on a downhill spiral. Wind and rain was becoming the main feature of each day. We went through Melick and Portumna without causing any damage to either and out onto Lough Derg. Marion wasn't too enamoured with the wind on the lake so we decided to go only as far as Portumna Castle Harbour. This is a sheltered harbour just at the very start of the lake. This meant that we would avoid getting bounced around in the strong winds. As it happened, while we were on the way into the harbour, Mar suggested that we by-pass Portumna and keep going further down the lake.

We avoided the worst of the weather by keeping in the lee of the land whenever possible and, a short time later, we navigated the short river-like entrance to Dromann Harbour on the County Clare shore. This is a beautiful harbour with ample berths. There is no town here but the harbour is surrounded by tall trees that act as a wind break for the picnic tables and stone BBQs that are scattered around. We were the only boat in the harbour and so we nestled down for a quiet evening. I took a walk along the lake shore in the hope that I would see another boat. I felt a bit like Robinson Crusoe and this feeling was made worse because I didn't see any other boats on the lake at all that day. Even the boat hire company in Portumna were advising their customers to stay off the lake and to go upriver instead because there was no sign of the wind abating. As the trees around the harbour emphasised the strength of the wind, we slept peacefully onboard *Driftwood*.

The morning brought no improvement in the weather. We moved to Scarif harbour because my Dad was joining us there and because it was a very sheltered harbour lying as it does up the Scarif River and about a mile or so in from the lake. Dad arrived at about 5pm. However, the wind was worse by then and we decided to wait until it died down in the evening. Unfortunately it didn't die down.

We were booked to go through Ardnacrusha Dam at seven in the morning so we had to move to Killaloe that night. We decided to give Mar the car, Dad and myself taking the boat.

We headed down the Scarif River and out into Lough Derg. It was dusk and the wind was scary. The only reason we decided to go was because we were booked for the dam. We had what sailors call a following sea, or what I call bloody big waves coming from behind us.

The further out from shore we got, the bigger the waves became. It's always a good idea to contact the coastguard and let them know the details of your trip. In the dark now I called them on the radio to let them know. "Do you know that there is a small craft warning?" came the reply. They were great, they contacted us every ten minutes to see where we were and if we were still happy with the weather. It was like having a big brother watching you. When we got into Killaloe I contacted them to say that we were tied up safely now. The man in the coastguard thanked us too.

I got into bed and pulled the quilt over my shoulders but the alarm went off. "What the hell is that?" I thought and looked at my watch. 5am? Where did the night go? I felt like I had been cheated by someone messing around with a time machine. Still, no good pondering the missing four hours' sleep. I got dressed in clothes that hardly had time to get cold. It was a bluey dawn, not as windy as the previous evening. Dad was up and dressed, and keen as mustard to get under way. My brother-in-law Noel, his wife Linda and their two children Amee and Keith arrived. I think they slept in the car, or maybe they got up before they went to bed.

This stage from Killaloe to Limerick is off limits to hire boaters but the *End of Navigation Notice* did not apply to us. We were adventurers, on an exploration, a quest to voyage into the unknown. At 5.30am we passed under Killaloe Bridge while all around us people slept.

Below Killaloe there is The Flooded Area. It's a lake that they forgot to name. They flooded a small parish when they built the dam back in the 1920s. There was an oratory on an island there. The local parishioners took it down stone by stone and carried it to higher ground in Ballina. There they rebuilt the small church. When the water came the parishioners lost their homes to it, as slowly the water got higher and higher until eventually the little houses sank beneath the surface, never to feel the air again.

As we sailed across the flooded area a single chimney pot watched us from just above the water line, like a periscope from a forgotten village, the ghosts of old villagers peering into the other end.

Up ahead the skyline was dominated by Parteen Villa Weir. This is a huge concrete structure that marks the start of the twelve-kilometre headrace leading to the dam itself. As we passed through the massive guillotine gate I got a 'no going back' feeling. We really are on our way to Limerick. The headrace took a full hour then we arrived at the dam. Like an iceberg, most of the dam is below the surface. There is a difference of one hundred feet between the upper and lower sides of the dam.

Ardnacrusha Dam was built by Siemens for the Electricity Supply Board back in the mid 1920s as a symbol of the new Republic which had been formed a few short years previously. At the time it produced one hundred percent of Ireland's electricity, now the figure is closer to two percent. Nonetheless, it is an overpowering and impressive structure. Boats pass through a double lock on the left-hand side of the dam. The first chamber lowers you sixty feet then you pass into the lower chamber to drop a further forty feet into tidal water where a great river and a great ocean meet.

Ger is the lock keeper in Ardnacrusha. He is a very obliging lad who told us: "I can lock you through any time once there is daylight, it doesn't matter how early." I was going to say that it gets bright at about 4.30am but thought better of it. We agreed on 7am to avoid the turbines. The turbines consume one hundred tonnes of water per second and there are four turbines. When running, each turbine creates one knot of current, lots of knots make a problem and, add to that an outgoing tide, and you could be swept away, never to be heard of again.

I had been advised that we would probably avoid the turbines by getting through the dam before 8am, and also that the ideal time to arrive in Limerick would be three hours before high tide, but it takes two hours to travel from Killaloe to Limerick and another hour to go through the dam. Don't get the timing wrong or you will surely breathe your last.

The bridges are low. When the tide comes in you can get stuck under them. Then the tide will rise further and crush your boat like a ball of tinfoil. Everyone inside will die. If you try to get out you will drown in the current. I considered bringing cyanide tablets so we wouldn't be taken alive. It would be the best thing if we all went together. All the advice was leading to information overload; I timed everything to the last second, I knew when to go to bed and when to get up, how long to spend in the bathroom, how long over breakfast. I think I was going mad but I hadn't allowed any time to think about that so I didn't dwell on it. But Ger puts you at your ease. He is just laid back and easy going. He locked us through and out the other side without any problems.

Limerick is a lovely city and from the river it is surprisingly attractive. We passed the island fields on our right, which the locals call "Dyland." I flew a Limerick flag so they wouldn't throw stones off the bridges on us, but as it happened they were still in bed.

Having safely passed under the bridges we tied up behind the Hunt Museum by the Farmers Tax Office, but we didn't see any farmers. I don't think anyone has ever seen a farmer at the Farmers Tax Office. Noel headed to work and Linda and Keith headed home to catch up on sleep. We slept too, then later Mar headed back to Dublin and my son Ben and my brother Aidan joined us in Limerick. This made us an all-male crew. You would think that we would be ready for anything, but the wind was howling outside and the weather forecast man was warning us about an 'Unsettled Airflow.' This is meteorological language for: "Don't blame us if the wind turns to gale force and you capsize in the storm."

I decided that a trip to Kilrush in the estuary would be more like work than relaxation so the following day we headed back upriver again and through the dam. Our foray into the brine was not going to go ahead and this was a pity because this was a sort of dip-your-feet-in-the-water exercise, only with a boat instead of a foot. This was to test how the boat would behave at sea so that next May I would have at least some experience when we tried to sail to France. Our retreat meant that we were

really going to be venturing blind the following year, with no
experience and no idea if the boat was able for the journey. Or
if we were able.

We returned back through the dam, across the flooded area,
and back to Killaloe. There we enjoyed a good meal and washed
it down a pint of the black stuff.

In Ireland we say that if the cows in the fields are sitting down,
it's a sign that it is going to rain soon, and if they're standing up
it means that it is raining. That morning they were sitting down
so we headed up Lough Derg, the Red Lake. We stopped in
Mountshannon for dinner, and the cows are still not standing
so we headed to the Mountshannon Hotel for a bite to eat.
Many years ago my two brothers, Aidan and Conor, as well
as my Dad and myself were in this hotel. It happened to be
our Dad's birthday so Aidan had secretly brought a cake. My
brother Conor kept Dad occupied while back by the kitchen
Aidan and myself cornered a young lounge girl. "Would you
bring out this cake to our Dad with the candles lighting?" we
asked her. She readily agreed so we upped the ante. "Would
you sing happy birthday as you walk through the lounge?"
We asked. "No way." She said. We did a bit of pleading and
promised her a hefty tip. Soon she agreed. Then we upped
the ante further by getting her to practice singing it under
the guise that our Dad was a singing instructor and she could
expect him to be quite fussy. "Can you up that an octave?" said
Aidan. She took a deep breath and tried again. "Oh E-flat,"
said Aidan, "that's beautiful. Oh he loves E-flat," I said, "it's
his favourite."

Once the rehearsals were over and we were happy with the quality of the singing, we returned to our seats, and a few minutes later the bar was struck silent by the sound of the lounge girl singing Happy Birthday, in E-flat, as she carried the cake across the lounge. It was terribly cruel of us but we did give her a sizeable tip by way of compensation. I worry when I recall incidents like that. They expose a darker side of my personality.

It wasn't anyone's birthday this time, so we had a pint and our dinner and hoped that the lounge girl wouldn't recognise us.

The cows stood up and rain returned for the afternoon and I soaked up a fair amount of it in my clothes as we progressed up the lake towards Portumna Harbour. It's just as well that skin is waterproof. We finished off the night in a local pub. We all had to go back to Dublin the next morning as work waits for no man. I only had to go back for a few days and fewer than my boss thinks.

Marion and myself returned to the boat on the following Thursday. The weather forecast that morning said that the rain would be more summery later in the day, with breaks in the showers to allow for longer spells of rain. We had had rain every day for thirty-two days. It was the wettest July since records began, and they began before Noah built that ark of his. Someone said that it had rained every day since the Green Party got into Government. Well, we needed someone to blame so why not those bloody Greens?

Between showers we went for a walk around the forest park in Portumna. There is a fortified house there. The tourist board call it a castle but it's not a real castle, just a big old house with battlements over the front porch. It costs €2.10 each to go into the house but you can stand outside in the rain for nothing. We went back to the boat because the man who does the tour hadn't got out of bed yet. Portumna has the best pub in Ireland. It is on the main street and it serves only Guinness. Other drinks are, of course, available but the Guinness is so good that no one drinks anything else. It's called Hayes's and Seamus pulls a pint with a religious reverence and respect normally only to be displayed for a visiting Pontiff. You haven't visited Portumna if you haven't visited Hayes's pub.

The harbour proved to be a fine structure with showers, toilets and washing machines. There was a hire boat beside us but we hadn't seen the occupants and it had been there all week. All their belongings were inside but there was no sign of life. Mar said that maybe they all fell in and nobody will report them missing until the boat becomes overdue. I thought that a little improbable, preferring to believe they had a pact and committed mass suicide in the back cabin. Either way we moved our boat to the next finger just so we won't be involved in the coroner's inquest.

A guy who sounded a lot like Borat was showing about twenty twelve-year-olds how to canoe and swim and to run in circles holding the paddle vertically over their heads while staring at the furthest point of the paddle and trying not to fall over. It would be a useful skill once they developed it. When they succumbed to dizziness Borat offered them a high five, but invariably the children preferred to lie in the wet grass and hold on to something immovable. I offered them bottles of fizzy orange and Coke, but Borat was a disciplinarian and wouldn't allow refreshments until they swam in the harbour and did the twirly thing with the paddle.

Someone should have told him about sea toilets. Fizzy drinks on an already tender stomach and probably combined with some harbour water is not a good idea. We thought we might have to move again. The smell became terrible. I hoped it wasn't the bodies in the hire boat.

The time came to say goodbye to Lough Derg and head north once again. Ironically there was no wind and as we sailed off the lake, our wash created the only waves in sight.

Shannon Bridge was full so we headed up the river Suck to Ballinasloe. We had never been up the river Suck before so this was another adventure. The first thing you notice about this river is that no one has bothered to straighten out all the bends so it has a tortuous course. You might see a boat across the fields on your right then twenty minutes later you pass the boat on your left. At first the landscape is bog, a fuel supply for the local power station in Shannon Bridge, then it becomes grazing land for cattle and, as you get closer to the town, the cattle give way to horses.

Everything about Ballinasloe is of an equine nature, either directly or indirectly. Horses just don't do it for me so I went for a haircut. I was also looking for a laundrette so when it was my turn for the young Polish girl to cut my hair I thought it would be a good idea to ask her where the nearest laundrette was. 'Machine?' She asked. "Yes" I said. "A washing machine." She picked up the hair trimming machine and got stuck into my hair like she was harvesting wheat. Just as well I like my hair tight. Then another woman who Mar had collared for an

impromptu gossip told her where to eat and wash the clothes
and what to see and where to moor the boat and how to make
leek and mushroom soup. We went to the café that had been
recommended to us by the lady. Normally it is a good idea
never to eat anything from any eatery that laminates its menus,
but the Bread Basket on the main square is an exception to this
rule. We ate well and it didn't cost the earth either.

There was a statue of a man in the town centre and he
was leading a horse. It doesn't mention his name but I think
I recognised him; he tried to tar-macadam my driveway a few
years back. That's the thing about Ballinasloe: it's very popular
with travellers. We moored at a nice hotel about a mile outside
the town and across the river from a dog food factory that smelt
pretty foul. However, it was mercifully far away from the noise
of the town. Evidently the dog food manufacturing process is
very smelly.

Next morning we moved north to Lanesboro and later that
evening we went in search of a good pub. In a bar close to the
harbour, a couple who had been there too long were shaping
up to each other. Piped music was blaring and the telly was in
your face even if you couldn't hear it over the music. Tellies
ruined our pubs. Nobody talks when there is a telly on, and
why can't you get a good old packet of King or Tayto crisps any
more? Why does it have to be Pringles? There's nothing wrong
with Pringles but I just long for the days when Irish pubs were
full of chat and it didn't cost the earth for some crisps. Don't
get me going about dry roasted peanuts, like there was such a
thing as a wet roasted ones, and then there are those tiny little
cardboard cups with a false bottom so the barman can sell you
a minute portion of *Hot Nuts* from a special nut heater on the
bar. I remember when hot nuts were what you got when you

had been cycling yer bike for too long. TVs, expensive snacks, and no chat, no wonder the good old Irish pub is in decline. We didn't have a second pint, choosing to go on a hunt for a better pub instead. Up the top of the town we found one and there was a guy the size of the alcove that he was sitting in, and he was singing Johnny Cash numbers with a voice that Johnny would be jealous of. He entertained us for the evening. Couples were up dancing jives together and one plonker was doing a jive on his own, having reached that point of intoxication when you think you are irresistible to the opposite sex and you really should go home. A forty-something Latvian with a big ten-gallon hat and an even bigger ego, who thought he was still twenty-one and was obviously in love with himself, was making many of the customers in the pub feel nauseous. Between Johnny's belly, the plonker's solo dancing and the Latvian lover's ego the pub was packed to bursting point, but the craic was good. Johnny Cash interrupted the music to announce that the Joe O'Reilly jury had just returned a guilty verdict. Joe O'Reilly was on trial for murdering his beautiful young wife and the whole nation had been captivated by the case. This was met with a round of applause and cheers, and Johnny commented that it was a sad day for Irish husbands who now could no longer kill our unco-operative wives. The partying continued unabated.

Chapter Two

The Atlantic beckons and the fools rush in

I SENT OFF A cheque to Lambay Sail Training in Malahide Yacht Club. It was late September 2007 and there was only eight months to my planned trip out into the sea and on to France. The course I was paying for was a Coastal Skippers course with the Royal Yachting Association. It is a basic course in navigation and it is designed to make you a useful member of a crew where you can gain experience and eventually go on to do a Yacht Masters course. I wouldn't be doing the Yacht Masters course or getting the experience bit they mentioned. I was jumping into the deep end.

My buddy Des was doing the course with me. He hoped to do some of the trip to France but hadn't worked out what he is going to tell his boss. I had been researching the French canals a lot on the net and had ordered some books to keep me busy. The French have a love of paperwork comparable with the Paddy's love of a pint of Guinness. I would need to get two boat licences, one for the fresh water and one for the salty stuff. I also needed registration documents for the boat. In Ireland no one bothers with such bureaucratic details. We favour a more relaxed system, in fact our system is so relaxed that we don't actually have a system at all. The French invented the word *bureaucracy* and so I had to go looking for VAT receipts and other scraps of paper that indicated that I owned my boat and hadn't stolen it somewhere.

I was trying to get a crew together but no one believed that I would get past Limerick. People sneered when I tried to bring up the subject. *"A man makes a reputation on what he has done, not on what he intends to do"* and I had done nothing like this before. No one was willing to take me seriously. It got so bad that I really had to ask myself: "Are they right? Maybe they are. Maybe I am a fool who has a stupid dream that will never come to anything." I analysed the trip in my mind. If I kept it to short five or six-hour hops it should be easy. I had no experience so was only guessing really.

We completed the course in April and I learnt a lot, and not just about navigation either. I learned about tides, headlands, and weather. There was no mention of tattoos.

"Who's taking the horse to France?" Mar scoffed as we drank pints in Liam Taylor's pub in Drumsna. "When Harry gets Alzheimer's I'll sit him in a rocking chair in the front room and with a basin at his feet, I'll splash water over him, rock the chair and say sure Harry you're half way cross the channel now." The crowd laughed aloud. I smiled and nodded but inside I promised myself that I would let nothing stand in my way. I was going to bring that bloody horse to France if it killed me. I sipped my pint, which was excellent, and the banter went on.

Liam's pub was voted the best pub on the river. There are no pretences here, no deep-pile carpet, no soft lighting and no hot nuts. But Taylors has a cosy honest atmosphere where you can enjoy a chat with decent company over a good pint and you can't say that about many pubs nowadays.

The sun was shining and it was decidedly warm when I untied and cast off from Albert Marina in Drumsna. It was here at last. The day had arrived and I didn't want to wait another hour. I really was going to sail to France. There was no one there to say farewell, no one to wish me good luck or wave a flag and so, alone on the boat, I slipped quietly out of the mooring. White water bubbled at the bow as I picked up speed and headed downriver bound for Limerick and the sea beyond.

My heart was full of determination. I had sailed every leg of the journey many, many times before as I lay dreaming in my bed. Now it wasn't a dream any more. I really was on my way. I was going to take the bloody horse to France.

I was enjoying the weather as well as the solitude. It contrasted well with the hustle and bustle of the past few days when I had been making last minute preparations for the trip. It seemed like a good idea to drop anchor in Lough Forbes and have a bit of grub and a nice cup of tea. A few boats passed by and looked curiously at the black ball hanging from my mast. This was one of the less important things that I had learned on the course. You are supposed to show a black ball on your mast when you're anchored. So I thought I would be very correct, and do the right thing. No one takes any heed of it here in Ireland where we have a well established disregard for all authority. As it happens it never got used again.

It amazed me how muddy the river bottom was so I decided to leave the anchor hanging just below the surface while I slowly drove the boat forwards to clean the mud off it. I suppose I must have gone a little faster than I had thought and this was my first mistake. The anchor finished up grand and clean but the depth sounder started acting up immediately. I knew the sensor for this device was at the front of the boat and it must have got a smack in the teeth with a mud-covered anchor. Depth sounders are useful items to have on a boat. If ever you run aground, a depth sounder will usually confirm the fact for you, so I suspected that this one might well be missed.

I dropped the radar mast to go under the bridge at Lanesborough and, as I emerged out the other side of the bridge, I switched on the auto pilot. The auto pilot keeps the boat on a straight course. I went up front and had just raised the mast when the boat swung violently to the right. I lost my footing and the mast fell down. Scrambling to the controls, I switched off the auto pilot, and only narrowly missed hitting the concrete jetty - much to the amusement of the local men fishing from the jetty at the time.

When I got into open water I slipped into neutral and went up front to see what damage was done to the mast and radar. The mast holder was bent badly and I could no longer raise the mast fully. In the autopsy I realised why the boat had swerved so violently when it should have maintained its course. The auto pilot is controlled by a fluxgate compass and it gets its course from this compass. Unfortunately this device is mounted half way up the mast and once I raised the mast I upset the compass. It was day one and I realised I had already broken the depth sounder, the mast and I might have damaged the radar too. Given that I expected to get to France in about three weeks, if I continued to break vital navigation equipment at the rate of two to three items per day we would surely all perish in the deep blue sea.

I crossed Lough Ree in great weather punctuated by occasional thunder showers. I tied up in Athlone to get a few cans of Guinness and a snack box. I shared the Off Licence with a guy who had a tattoo of a swallow on the side of his neck and a few more just to complete his accessorising. The tattoo man jumped the queue and I didn't object. He looked like he had just given the Emergency Response Unit the slip and anyway he had to buy ten cans of Newcastle Lager at €1 each because Manchester United was playing Barcelona, or something like that. I bought my Guinness and was relieved that Tattoo man didn't steal my bike. After getting a tasty snack box I fired up the engines and headed off again.

I stopped in Shannon Bridge because I was feeling tired and wanted to rest up and the pace of life there is very appropriate. Shannon Bridge boasts one of the best pubs on the river, Killean's of Shannon Bridge. They say that when the shelves behind the counter no longer appear to be at an angle you have had enough and it's time to go home. I wasn't to visit Killean's on this occasion.

After a rest it was time to move on to Banagher, where craíc and music in J.J. Hough's awaited. The following morning I headed to Heidi's café where you're always assured of a good breakfast. I know Heidi of old and we had a chat over a cup of tea. I told her I was on my way to France in my boat and she said "Oh that's nice," and she finished her cup of tea.

Later I was joined by a friend of mine, Tony O'Connor. Tony has his own boat on the river and his company was a pleasant change from the solitude. We cruised in lovely early summer sunshine down the meandering silver path that is the southern Shannon. At Portumna we had to wait for the swing bridge to open. The bridge carries a main road and when it opens to allow boats to pass through, almost all the road traffic in or around Portumna grinds to a halt. Things then usually remain quite stagnant until the bridge swings closed again and normal traffic flow can resume.

We tied onto a hotel barge that was big enough to be called a ship. We had the impression that it was cunningly designed to make it close on impossible to tie alongside. A determined crew can manage to do it and we were determined. "Can we walk across your barge?" I asked the woman who had an air about her as though she might be in charge of something. After she looked us up and down to see if we were up to standards she said: "Well only if your shoes are clean." We looked at each other and then we looked at our shoes, then we looked at each other's shoes, then we looked at her and we could see that she was not joking. She escorted us through the floating hotel's dining room, keeping a careful watch in case we robbed the silverware or some cutlery.

Once we were safely escorted onto the quayside we headed to the pub for a pint and a sandwich and to splash in some puddles on our way back.

When the bridge slowly swung open we passed through. Holding up so much traffic for so long can give you a certain power rush. Once through the bridge you are at the most northerly point of Lough Derg. It's a beautiful lake when it is not doing an impersonation of the Southern Ocean. It is about thirty kilometres long and thirteen kilometres wide at its widest point, so it's not a lake to be messed with. Thankfully it was behaving itself. Tony and myself cruised south, taking in the scenery along the way. We were heading for Garrykennedy, a town only just large enough to qualify for its very own name. It has two pubs, which is the minimum requirement for any Irish town, and both of them are good, which is certainly not a requirement. The moorings have been improved here in recent years and you no longer have to raft a dozen boats out and listen to the whining of the skipper on the inside who has been stuck there since last April.

Marion prevented us from going to the pub by being at the jetty before us. Tony had to head home because his wife thought that he was out the back cutting the grass and he could be caught out at any moment. We said our farewells and he wished me good luck on the voyage.

The next morning the weather was still fine. I brought the boat to Killaloe while Marion drove the car to meet me there. Here in Killaloe we were joining a number of other boats and we would all cruise into Limerick together. It was Friday, May 2 and the start of the Bank Holiday weekend.

In every group of people there is one person who stands out as a leader. It's never me. On this occasion it was Fergal. I knew Fergal of old. However, I hadn't seen him for several years. He proved just as methodical, meticulous, and exacting as ever. If you want a job done, get Fergal to do it. That way you know that the task will be executed with military precision. The meeting, and there is always a meeting, was called for 7pm, and it got under way at the stroke of 8.30pm. Fergal explained the hazards of the trip into Limerick and, to be fair, it is a trip you need to plan for. When the meeting was over we synchronised our watches, swore a blood oath, then under the cover of darkness, we returned to our own boats.

There were five boats there and we planned to leave Killaloe in two groups, the first group at 8am and the second one an hour later. We were in the group that didn't get a lie-in. That didn't bother me; I was excited about the trip into Limerick and, unlike last year, this time we would get out to sea. That night marked the end of the laid-back waterways. Ahead lay adventure, danger and the unknown.

We untied and cast off right on schedule. Noel and his wife Linda and their two teenage children Amee and Keith had joined us again for the trip into Limerick. I loved this trip; Limerick is the jewel in the crown of the River Shannon. Few boats visit it although that is starting to change. The moorings behind the Hunt Museum are superb. They offer security as well as a hook-up for electricity and a great view of King John's Castle, which dominates this part of the city. Everything you need is available within a short walk and at night when you have finished up swamping creamy pints in Locks Bar or some other hostelry, you can return to the peace and quiet of your mooring where your boat cannot even be seen from the shore.

We headed across the flooded area, three boats in the first group, *Reflection*, a Dutch steel cruiser skippered by Richard, is like my own only a lot newer and a bit bigger too. Then there was *Firefly,* a fibreglass cruiser about nineteen feet long crewed by Denise, with some help from Paul, a family friend.

Reflection was first into the huge lock at Ardnacrusha Dam, *Firefly* fitted in beside him and then we squeezed in behind. You probably could have fitted another boat in if you tried hard enough but it's best to allow some room for manoeuvre on the long descent. Ger, the lock keeper, recognised us from last year and Mar gave him a sandwich of sausages, rashers, pudding and a fried egg. Ger ate the sandwich and bravely carried on as though there were no increased risk to his hart.

The huge guillotine gate dropped behind us and sealed us in. Down we went, slowly bit by bit. The patch of sky grew smaller and smaller above us. It was like looking up out of a grave. Still further down we descended, until it all stopped, and then another guillotine gate in front of us lifted up. With water dripping down from the gate, the two boats in front started to move forward. It looked like they were entering the mouth of an enormous monster, dripping with saliva. The monster didn't eat them so we followed on into the second chamber. This one was to drop us the final forty feet to sea level.

When you exit Ardnacrusha lock the first thing you notice is that it is a most beautiful location. Trees overhang the river and we gently cruised along, getting closer and closer to Limerick city. We passed *Dyland* and into the section known as the Abbey River. It's here that Limerick first comes into view, and what a view. If you haven't been to Limerick by boat make sure to do it before you die. It's possibly not as good doing it when you're dead.

That bank holiday weekend the city was buzzing. The World BBQ championships were taking place so the smell of food was mouth-watering, although you would wonder how some of them made it to the finals because most of the burgers and sausages we got were only half-cooked. In the end I went to a good Turkish fast-food near the market where I enjoyed a super doner kebab.

On the Sunday there was a French market. That's got to be a good omen, I thought. Here I learnt that the French are not shy. I'm the sort of guy who falls head over heels for the hard sell. I can't resist. I don't want to be offensive. It's so much easier to just buy whatever they are selling. I spent €35 on olives that I couldn't eat and as much again on cheese - enough to feed a small army.

Jack, a local sailor, came to check out my boat. "I heard you are planning to sail to France?" "Yes," I said. "Oh very dodgy thing to do. You been to sea much?" He asked. "No never before actually." "This boat doesn't look like it's up to the job. I've been in hurricanes you know." "You could never tell." I said. "Oh you will see some waves out there in the Atlantic you know. Your grab rail doesn't feel very secure." By now he is hanging by both arms with his legs dangling beneath him. "Bet if I swung out of this and gave it a good smack with that hammer it would break. It's not up to the job. You will never get to France. You haven't a clue about the sea. Did I tell you that I sailed in the Pacific?" "No not yet." I said. "See that table? You didn't even secure it to the floor." "I might want to move it." I said. "Ha, move it? The sea will move it for ya. You need to screw that into the floor with three-inch screws. In fact I'm going to get you the screws myself. You really don't have a clue you poor fool. Hope you're insured. You're going to need it." "I

am insured." I said. "What?...How did you get insurance? It's
no wonder that our policies are going up all the time. Are you
bringing an estuary pilot?" he asked. "No." I said. "See what
I mean? You're clueless; no one goes out the estuary without a
pilot on board. You are all going to drown, there is no doubt
about it. You will all die in this useless old boat. Did I mention
that I was in a hurricane?" "You did Jack." I said. You sleep
better after a few words of encouragement.

On Sunday evening my eldest son Ben arrived from nearby
Ennis, where he lives. The two of us planned to head up the
estuary to Kilrush about four hours away. We said farewell
to Marion, who was going to take the car to Kilrush. Paul
arrived along just before we untied. "Thought I'd take some
photographs?" "Thanks Paul," I said. They will probably help
in identifying our bodies later.

At 8:55am on Monday, May 5, 2008, the gates in the sea lock
at Limerick slowly opened. As they did they exposed the brine,
that formidable barrier. Ahead lay the Shannon Estuary and
the wild Atlantic Ocean beyond and somewhere out there,
there is a country called France and my El Dorado. Paul took
photos from the shore, young girls waved from the bridge and
I think I saw some of them wipe away a tear, and then some of
them shouted: "Bring us back a parrot." The band played 'Oh
Solo Mio' and the Twelfth Battalion from Sarsfield Barracks
gave us a gun salute, as the lads from The Munster Rugby
team punched the air. "Good on ye lads," they shouted. Ronan
O'Gara stepped forward: "You will make the whole country
proud lads." Then Peter Stringer shoved his way to the front.
"We love you guys, you're heroes," he yelled. Then we slipped

out into the great blue yonder, waving to the crowds as we passed by.

Well….. at least the lock keeper said: "Good luck lads, yez feckin eejits."

Chapter Three

Beginners' Luck

THE ESTUARY IS where the ducks and swans of the inland waterways give way to seagulls and gannets of the oceans. I became suddenly aware that this was serious stuff.

Ben took the wheel and we passed beneath the new bridge. This was the last bridge we would pass under as there are no bridges at sea. Because we had to drop the radar mast at most Shannon bridges, I had seldom used the four stainless steel cables provided to secure it in place, but now things had changed. For the first time since I bought *Driftwood* I had to secure the mast properly. As I did so I became acutely aware of the significance of this: when would I remove the cables again? When the boat was being put on a low loader at Fenit to return to the Shannon in shame? Or could we just possibly, actually make it to France? The likelihood seemed slight. Quietly, I was not very confident of success; in fact I had only bought charts to cover the coast as far south as Cork. I didn't want to waste money on charts that we may never need.

There was a force six wind forecast but as it was due to come from the south, this meant that it would be blowing across the estuary and wouldn't be much of a problem to us. We passed the Ball of Whelps green marker, a five-meter high tower like a small electricity pylon. As we slipped by the outgoing tide ripped around its legs. The tidal current in the estuary should never be underestimated and we had timed our departure to take full advantage of its mighty power. Fergus Rock Red, Bridge Green, Conor's Rock Red and Carrick Bank Green: I carefully ticked every marker off from a list I had drawn up. It's easy to get confused or to mistake one of the old channel markers for a new one and end up going over a mud flat or a shoal. I was being meticulously careful.

The wind picked up just as we passed Shannon Airport and, as luck would have it, this is where the estuary opens up and starts to become exposed. We pressed on and Beevs Rock Lighthouse came into view up ahead in the distance. We gave it a wide berth as the shoal extends well out from it. Then, swinging north east, we approached Aughinish Island.

We passed the terminal at Aughinish Island and saw the first seagoing ship we came across, *The Faviola*. She was tied up and unloading her cargo.

The river narrows again at this point and the current really picks up as you pass Foynes Island and approach Tarbert. This is the place where the ferries cross and avoiding them was easier than I had expected and they helped by giving way to us. We saw our first dolphins jump out of the water here but I was too preoccupied trying to avoid the ferries to take a photo of them.

Just opposite Money Point there is a bank in the centre of the river called The Bridge. We passed to its south and then swung North. Taking a bearing of 310 degrees true, we held this course for about two-and-a-half miles and it led us into Hog Island sound. In the sound the tide was making a lot of white water, "Overfalls" is what people who know about these things call it, but just beyond it was calm again. We held on and in we went, rockin'n rollin here, we bounced about a bit and a few minutes later we were out the other side and there in front of us was the line of markers leading us into Kilrush Marina.

We lined up the two leading marks on the shore and followed the line to the lock that leads into the marina. It's a great feeling to successfully navigate the first leg. When we tied up in the marina Marion was waiting on the shore. After some grub she and Ben headed away and I stayed with the boat waiting for my crew to arrive.

The Bus Eirean bus from Limerick pulled into the stop outside the draper's shop in Kilrush and a few people stepped off carrying bags from Dunnes Stores, but no one had any goats, livestock, or wicker baskets with live chickens. Then a well-built man stepped off the bus, walked up to me and shook my hand firmly: "I'm Malachy. You must be Harry." "Where is my Dad?" I asked as they were supposed to travel together and there was no sign of him. "Ah we had a bit of a disagreement and he went and sat at the back of the bus." Then a broad grin betrayed Malachy's hearty sense of humour and Dad emerged from the bus smiling. We collected the bags and stacked them on a small two-wheeled trolley and we walked the half mile or so to the boat. On the way one of the bags fell off the trolley just as we were crossing the road and a carton of soya milk burst open and most of the contents of the bag spilled out onto the road. All the traffic had to stop and wait while we picked everything up, then we continued on our way and the cars moved on again.

When we got to the boat I had soup and sandwiches ready for the troops.

I had planned that we would only travel for about five to seven hours each day because I wanted the trip to be a pleasure cruise, not an endurance test. As it turned out we had to put in much longer days. The plan for eating was that we would have a breakfast of cereal, eggs and toast, or something similar, on the boat. We would have lunch on the move and it would come out of a tin or a packet. But then each evening we would go ashore and have a proper meal in a pub or restaurant.

I explained my plan for the trip to Fenit in Co Kerry. We would move on that evening and overnight in the lock at the entrance to Kilrush harbour. That way we could be away early in the morning with the tide behind us.

I was uneasy about the forecast; the wind was easterly force five. Normally this would be my cue to tie up the boat and go to the pub, but I had spoken to a local and he said that these were near perfect conditions, "Sure you never get an offshore wind like this on the west coast. Jesus, if you can't get to Fenit in this weather you may turn around and go back to the Shannon 'cos you'll never get there." The words kept repeating in my head. Always trust local knowledge they say. Later that evening when the last of the yachts had returned we entered the lock and the lock keeper lowered the water and then opened the lower gates. There we stayed. The wind was unceasing and then the forecast said it would increase to a force six, a small craft warning was given too. Feeling very unsure about this I went back to my friend with the latest forecast, only to be told again: "For God's sake, it's an offshore wind. If you can't get there in that weather you will never get there."

I didn't sleep much that night. The wind whistled and the boat banged as it rattled about in the lock on slack ropes to allow for the rising tide. At first light I got up and looked around. The wind was blowing incessantly, the knot in my gut had formed itself into a bowline with a couple of half hitches thrown in for good measure. It wasn't high water just yet, so we had to wait another while. The mood of the sea is dictated by the winds and the tides. Two factors over which no man has control.

As others were asleep in their beds, or maybe getting up for work, we fired up the engines and headed out past Scattery Island. We took a heading of 249 degrees for Kilcredaun Point.

Not everyone who wants to go on an adventure like this can manage to do it. But for those who cannot, I carried their dreams of adventure with me, they were on board too, like a cargo that I would carry with me all the way to France.

Driftwood rose up on the swells as if she was enjoying herself. Up and down we went, sometimes a little sideways motion but not too uncomfortable. At the Kilcredaun point we headed in a more south-westerly direction to take us to a position just off Kerry head. It was getting lumpier now, with plenty of white caps on the waves. On we went but the rocking was greater than any I had experienced before. When the Ballybunion north cardinal marker was off to our right, or starboard side,

I decided to change the plan and point us into the waves. This put us on a south-easterly course and we were heading straight for Ballybunion. My idea was to get closer to the shore and that way avoid the worst of the waves. It worked with limited success. We followed along the Kerry coast, keeping out around Cashen Spit and on all the way to that spot where Kerry head rushes down to meet the sea. I have heard it said since that it is always rough around Kerry head. I don't know if that's true but it certainly was rough that day.

As we rounded the head we met the weather full on. We came down off waves and the nose of the boat buried itself into the next wave before rising up again, sending salt water everywhere. I didn't know who it was that welded this boat together, but I was thinking of them then, and I hoped to God that they had made a good job of it.

Our course was now 190 degrees almost due south. The waves were relentless and occasionally you would get an extra large one that would cause you to hold on tight, white knuckles all round. I was not sure what we could do if our engines failed in these conditions. I just hoped that they would keep going. I suppose this was a baptism of fire, but I promised myself at the time that I was not going to suffer this all the way to France. I was going to have to rethink the whole voyage. Had I bitten off more than I could chew?

After an age the mighty outcrop they call Mucklamore Rock came into view and this was a welcome sight because I was beginning to think we were stationary for the past hour. It wasn't that you could use it as any kind of safe haven, it was simply evidence that we were getting closer to Fenit and the shelter of a good harbour.

We passed to the west of Mucklamore and the sea became less aggressive. Little Samphire Island guards the entrance to Fenit harbour, backed up by a statue of St Brendan the Navigator on Great Samphire that now forms part of the harbour itself. As we entered the harbour I felt a great sense of relief. We tied up and Malachy exclaimed that a big plate of bacon and cabbage with loads of spuds would hit the spot nicely.

I went up to the Harbour Master's office where a pretty young black girl was sorting through the paperwork. I filled out a form and asked her if she knew any where around that might serve bacon and cabbage? "Bacon and cabbage," she shouted at me, in a soft Anglo-Kerry accent. "Go home to your mother if it's bacon and cabbage you want. This is a fishing port and you'll eat fish here same as everyone else." You cannot salvage your character after something like that. I meekly headed back to tell Malachy he wasn't getting any bacon and cabbage that day. We went to the pub and avoided the steak sandwich, opting for a fish dinner, just in case the black girl appeared and scolded us for not eating the local produce.

I went to bed that night with a peaceful mind. I now knew that if the wind came up I would have no hesitation in pulling the plug on the day's planned trip. The trip to Fenit taught me to trust my own judgment and not to go against it. As it turned out we woke to the sound of no sound: The wind had stopped and soon the sea area forecast confirmed our hopes. "Thunderbirds are go," and these thunderbirds were off to Dingle.

In beautiful sunshine and flanked by the mountains surrounding Tralee Bay, we headed around the Little Samphire Lighthouse and soon we set a course to take us through the Magharee sound off Rough Point. Thankfully that day Rough Point didn't live up to its name, but I would not like to have been here the previous day.

The scenery was beyond description - powerful rugged and unmerciful cliff faces off the port bow provided the backdrop to the commanding Atlantic swells, the surface of which had an oily smoothness. Still the swells lifted us up high and then slowly lowered us again. The more beautiful and the more rugged and the more dramatic the coastline, the more dangerous it is too.

The tranquillity was broken by a splash of something beside the boat. A large finned monster stirred just below the surface and reluctantly swam away from us. Two fins that broke the surface identified the first of two basking sharks we were to see that day. The sharks weren't the main attraction though. Even the scenery was pipped at the post by three bottlenose dolphins who rode our bow wave for about ten or fifteen minutes. They allowed us to film and photograph them as we hung over the bow and could almost touch them. These beautiful creatures are a sight I will forever remember and will recall at times when things are not as good as they were that day and I know that the memory will lift my spirits again.

The knot I had in my stomach the previous day had now been replaced by butterflies; dolphins have that effect on people.

We passed Smerwick Harbour, a natural harbour off on our portside, and Syble point lay up ahead. One of the main obstacles along the west coast of Ireland is the Blasket Sound. This narrow channel between Great Blasket and the Dunmore

Head is fraught with hazards. From the sea it is nigh on impossible to identify each of the rocks that shoot up from the bottom and pierce the surface. Even Youngs Island and the larger Beginish Island are hard to identify from the chart. It was Malachy who finally made a positive identification of Beginish, which the chart showed to be some thirteen metres high, making it the highest obstacle in the sound.

Rocks abound, Kilbreeda rock, Conor rock, Edge rock, and the tidal currents prevent a slow boat like ours from having any effective steering when the surge tries to squeeze through this narrow funnel. To avoid this we planned to arrive at the sound just before slack water, the point when a tide turns and allows a brief moment when this enormous mass of water becomes stationary. This gave us our window of opportunity and with the excellent weather we had, the trip through the sound was a breathtaking experience.

Even with these perfect conditions we met some fairly large swells at the southern end of the sound off Garraun Point and had the only green water of the day come over the decks.

On leaving the sound another lazy basking shark swam sluggishly beside the boat showing us his awesome bulk.
Soon we were heading east with Mount Brandon on our port side. Some more dolphins showed themselves before we got to Dingle. "Ye would get fed up of looking at those bloody dolphins wouldn't ye?" said Malachy with a touch of cynicism.

Fungi is also known as the *Dingle Dolphin*. People come from all corners to see this exceptionally friendly creature. We were chuffed because he escorted us into Dingle as a 'dolphin watch' boat filled with camera-clicking tourists followed us close behind.

Malachy was getting the bus to Tralee from Dingle and the train from there to Dublin. Unfortunately he had other commitments. He bought us lunch and a pint before his departure and he was missed as a humorous and enthusiastic member of the team.

Dad and myself untied from our mooring in Dingle at 8am the next morning and headed out into Dingle Bay. There was no sign of any dolphins that day and the large Atlantic swells made a forceful presence as we took a bearing to Skellig Michael, helped by a stiffening easterly wind. An hour later we decided to change our course and headed into Valentia as the sea had become too lumpy to continue.

You have to line up two leading red marks on the shore and then keep them in line as you enter Valentia. It's difficult to do when only one of the marks is visible. I presumed someone had robbed the second one and I imagined it was probably for sale on the black-market for leading marks. Then, just at the last minute, and as if by magic, the second leading mark came into view after all. I lined them up and forced the last few horsepower out of the diesels to try to keep a straight course through the narrow channel.

Beginish Island was on our left as we entered, and there is a pilot tower on it. The view of oncoming traffic was limited. Then, as if by design, a lobster boat came around the island. With nowhere to go, it looked like a major maritime disaster was about to unfold. The skipper of the lobster boat probably knew every rock in the channel and seemed to completely disregard the leading marks. He motored past us with a wave of his hand and across what I thought was a reef guaranteed to bring a miserable death to anyone who ventured too close.

We headed up to Cahirsiveen and tied up in the marina. This is a very sheltered harbour and we could feel none of the wind that had been such a problem to us in the bay. I wondered if I should have kept going to Derrynane. We went up to the town to send some postcards and as we returned to the boat it was clear that the wind had increased considerably. It looked like I had been exonerated in my decision to change course.

At 4am the alarm went off. I didn't know what it was at first so I got out of bed and put on some trousers. Dad got up at the same time. After all it was his idea to get up this early to beat the wind. After breakfast and while it was still dark we slipped our moorings in Cahirsiveen and headed down the short estuary flanked by flashing green and red markers. We were leaving at low tide and would have to battle the tide for the next six hours. We came out at Beginish Island just as it was getting bright; this time we cut the corner by going behind the island. The Irish coastguard radio station was clearly visible on nearby Valentia Island. It was from Valentia Island that Marconi made his first successful transatlantic radio transmission.

I radioed the coastguard and gave them details of our planned passage for the morning and in return they gave us the forecast of force three to four east to north east winds. At that moment there was no wind at all, but as we left the shelter of Bolus Head the Atlantic swells met us as if to say we're still here, wind or no wind. We took a bearing that pointed us towards Skellig Michael.

We climbed up and slid down the swells until about an hour later we had got around Valentia Island, then the coast moved away to our left and the sea calmed a bit. This was the first lesson we learned that day: keep off the coast, the water is calmer where you don't have waves bouncing back off the cliff face.

The Skellig Rocks are an awesome sight, especially at dawn. It's hard to imagine the life that monks once led on these barren rocky outcrops. Their beehive huts are still there to this day, including one solitary hut on the summit of Skellig Michael. With no trees, they must have only had a fire on occasions when turf was brought from the mainland and that cannot have been very often. I hope their God appreciated their sacrifice. I took some photographs and I also sent some to friends on my phone, not realising that it was about 6am on a Sunday morning and so they didn't attract the rapturous response I had hoped for.

The weather was holding so we decided to bypass Derrynane and head to the Dursey Sound instead. Dursey Island and the mainland appeared to blend into one as we approached. There was no sign of the channel that we had to pass through. We scanned the shoreline ahead of us and then chose one valley that appeared slightly more distinct than the others. We set a course for it and then, as we drew closer, the cable car that crosses the sound and brings the inhabitants as well as visitors to the island, came into view.

The rocks they call the Bull, the Cow and the Calf appeared off to our right, as the Skelligs started to fade into the morning mist. As we got close to the north entrance of the sound the eye in the bull became visible. I am told that you can pass through it in a dingy if you're brave enough or stupid enough.

We entered the sound doing just over seven knots and, as we went in the cable car crossed overhead. I sounded the horn and we waved at the people but no one waved back.

You have to keep to the right in Dursey Sound because there is a submerged rock mid-channel. The budget for the Irish Coastguard does not stretch to putting a marker on it.

We exited the sound and the sea became even calmer. We thought "let's give Bear Island a miss too," and so we set a course for Mizen Head some two hours away, across some of the most exposed water along the Irish coast. A basking shark showed himself long enough for us to capture him on video and get some still photographs too. We headed on with only slight swells betraying the presence of the world's second largest ocean.

We were listening to a mountain rescue on the VHF. A helicopter was called in to airlift a sixty-seven-year-old woman off the Kerry Mountains with a broken leg. "That's ridiculous," said Dad. "What was she doing, up a mountain at sixty-seven years of age?" "Look who's talking," I said. "You're seventy-three and you're out in the Atlantic in a small boat." "Yes I suppose I am," said Dad. "But the difference is that I don't feel like I'm seventy-three."

A single yacht running on its engine because there wasn't enough wind to sail by, passed us and we swopped waves and smiles, then we continued on. The Bull and its offspring disappeared into the mist as Mizen head came into view. The weather was great and already we were well ahead of schedule but I was also aware that it was about here that Charlie Haughey lost his boat and nearly his life too when his yacht Taurima was driven ashore during a storm in September, 1985.

It was mid-afternoon by the time we got to Crookhaven and we decided to call in to see if we could replenish our diesel. There was no diesel in Crookhaven but we enjoyed a coffee on the quayside in The Crookhaven Inn just the same. Later we headed a mile or so along the coast to a beautiful spot called Goleen. Here we tied to a new concrete jetty and I climbed the ladder with two gerry cans and headed to the town a short walk away.

Denny O'Meara's Pub on the corner sells green diesel from a tank in the farmyard round the back, if you don't mind a nosey and somewhat antisocial horse trying to bite you as you fill the cans from a hose that only trickles diesel at a pace slower then an old man having a pee.

Laura is one of the owners of Denny's and she lent me her car, complete with bales of straw, (I think chickens lived in it up until quite recently) to deliver the gerry cans to the boat. The whole operation went on for about two-and-a-half hours before I drained their diesel supply. This diesel was later to be a suspect when things went belly-up, but it was ultimately vindicated.

We left Goleen and headed off into a slight mist out around Cape Clear. As we did so the Fastnet Lighthouse loomed up from the glassy water and peered at us through the mist. We were on a new heading now on our way to Glandore bay. The sea was flat calm and the mist was slowly getting burnt off in the late afternoon sun.

We passed on the inside of the rocks they call The Stags. It is on these rocks that the world's largest ship wreck (by tonnage) took place. Beneath these waters there is a huge ship for this is where the wreck of the Kowloon Bridge lies. In November 1986, after crossing the Atlantic, the crew of the Kowloon Bridge noticed cracks in the decking. She made for Bantry Bay, where she anchored to make an assessment of the damage. However, shortly after leaving Bantry Bay she lost her steering and she eventually floundered on Stag Rock. All her crew were winched to safety but the cargo of 165,000 tones of iron ore went to the bottom while about 2,000 tones of fuel oil ended up on the coastline. The ensuing ecological disaster took a huge toll on wildlife. I had dived on this wreck about seven or eight years earlier and the memory always remained with me.

After passing outside High Island and Rabbit Island, Adam Island peered through the mist just outside Glandore Bay. Giving this island a wide berth, we passed close to Eve Island and into Glandore Bay as the cruising guide advised. This is a beautiful bay and it was complemented by beautiful weather. Inland boaters are spoilt with good moorings on the rivers, normally either floating jetties or solid concrete jetties. The sea-going fraternity are not accustomed to such luxuries and often have to make do with a mooring buoy. This was the case in Glandore bay. For the first time we had to use one of these mooring buoys. The first thing you realize is that it is extremely difficult to pick one up with a boat hook. Using prearranged hand signals I aimed the boat at a target that I could not see while my Dad waved his arms about like someone trying to deflect a wasp. After several buoy drive-bys we succeeded in hooking it. I have become a big fan of mooring buoys since they provide a certain solitude and privacy and they are away from the madding crowd. Once safely tied up we launched the rib and headed ashore where we enjoyed a good meal in a local watering hole. Later we returned to the tranquillity of the boat.

We awoke to glorious sunshine and enjoyed breakfast on the back deck while watching the view swing around us. A mild breeze had picked up as we slipped the mooring buoy that had been our port for the night and headed out into the bay and the open sea beyond.

It was Monday and we set a course for Crosshaven in the mouth of Cork harbour. Despite the wind there was still a mist and it was not always possible to see the shore a few miles away. We had set a direct course which would keep us well out to sea and this meant that only the headlands were really clearly visible. When the Old Head of Kinsale came into view my thoughts suddenly were of the men, women and children aboard the Lusitania. When she was torpedoed in the spring of 1915, she went to the bottom in just eighteen minutes and 1,198 people perished in this watery grave. Many of them could see the old Head of Kinsale lighthouse before they died.

Dad was feeling tired and lay down in the front cabin for a snooze. Shortly after that the weather forecast on the VHF told us that there was an easterly force four heading our way and, sooner than expected, it hit us nose-on. The contrast with the glassy calm water we had experienced earlier was quite distinct. As the bow rose and fell into the swells Dad slept on totally unaware of the weather change. He's a hardy old sea dog with salt water running through his veins. It comes from years of caravanning I suppose.

We rounded the Old Head while keeping well out from it and land went out of sight once again. A short time later an Irish

Naval vessel, probably the *LÉ Emer,* passed us on our port or left hand side ... at least I think port is left.

We carried on to the red marker just off Daunt Rock south of Cork harbour. Entering the bay there was a large ship, *The Shannon Fisher,* at anchor and we passed behind it. The markers at the entrance to Cork Harbour are confusing. I had expected the entrance to be reasonably straight but it's not. It doesn't matter too much when your draft is only one metre, but keeping out of the way of the large commercial traffic is a must.

We rounded Rams Head with Fort Davis (formerly Fort Camden) on one side of us and Fort Meagher (formerly Fort Carlisle) on the other. Both these forts were held by the British Crown until they were handed over to the Irish government in 1938, some sixteen years after we got independence.

The first mooring we came to was Crosshaven Boatyard and Marina so we tied up there and got a meal in a local Chinese restaurant. It was here in Crosshaven Boatyard that I met Donal and it was as a result of that chance meeting that our planned route was turned upside-down.

The first thing you notice about Donal is that he is a big man. The second thing you notice is that he loves boats and all things boat-related. Thirdly, he enjoys helping people. But mostly you notice that he's a big man.

Donal is very knowledgeable and he has plenty of yachting experience to draw on. I, on the other hand, am not so knowledgeable and had only the experience of the last four days to draw on. I had planned to continue up the coast as far as Kilmore Quay and from there, cross the Irish Sea at one of the shortest crossing points to Milford Haven in Wales. Crossing the sea here would take about nine and-a-half-hours. Then the plan was to cross the Bristol Channel and follow the English coast-line as far as Dover, where I would cross to Calais.

When I told Donal of my plan he said: "Harry if you don't mind me saying it, you're completely mad to go that route." "But what other route is there?" I asked.

Donal took a deep breath and then paused for effect, then he spun in his swivel seat and looked me in the eye. "If it were me," he said, "I'd go straight from here to Long Ships Lighthouse off Lands End and then to Newlyn in Cornwall, then cross the channel from Weymouth to Cherbourg and enter the French inland waterways at Le Havre." I was stuck for words. This was real yachty stuff he was talking. "What," I said "Go straight across the sea? That would take days, and this is an inshore boat if not a river boat." "You have two engines don't you?" said Donal. "Yes but she still only manages seven to eight knots." "Well let's see how long it would take at seven knots." We went onto Google Earth and drew the route. It was simply a straight line across the Celtic Sea all the way to Newlyn just around Lands End. Google Earth calculated it at 156 Nautical miles, that's about 180 statute miles or more importantly twenty-two hours and twenty minutes of gut knots.

I explained that I wasn't in a hurry and going that far from land was not the stuff for me. Then Donal did some maths and worked out that his route cut about three hundred miles off the trip. "That's a lot of diesel, and it's about another forty hours of boating - all of which has to be in good weather." He was starting to make sense. To go this new route would be much quicker but it required a decent twenty-four hour weather window. A search of internet weather sites showed just such a window in four days' time on Friday May 16.

I went back to the boat. "Dad, listen up. I need you to give me your honest opinion on this…" I related the conversation with Donal. After much thought and debate we both agreed that we would go with the new plan. There was nothing for it but to get a train home to Dublin and return the following Thursday evening. This also gave me time to get the charts I would need and to plan the course.

Chapter Four

Our Nemesis The Celtic Sea

MY WIFE MARION and my mother travelled back to Cork with us and we were joined later that evening by my brother Aidan.

The plan was for Aidan to accompany us to France and he had just one week to do it. We settled in for the night and we were all looking forward to tomorrow's trip, even if we were a little apprehensive. So far the forecast was good. The Met Office was predicting a force two to three, gusting force four, and dropping to a force two later in the day. I decided to check with Donal in the boatyard the following morning and we also planned to have a look at a few weather websites before leaving. I hoped Donal would show up early because we would have to leave at 9:45am in order to arrive at Longships lighthouse just before dawn.

I woke early on that Friday morning keen to ensure everything was in order for the long trip. As it happened the wind was very light. At 7am we all listened attentively to the latest forecast: there was no change from the previous day so once again it's "Thunderbirds are Go".

Paul, who we had last seen in Limerick, came along to film us as we left Irish shores behind. Mum and Marion were a bit apprehensive when I told them that Donal wouldn't be in on time for me to check the weather websites before we left, but I reassured them that there was no need to worry as the forecast from the coastguard was sufficient. Our water tank was full, so was the diesel tank and we had an extra one hundred-and-fifty litres of diesel in jerry cans strapped into the bilge if we needed them. I had changed the fuel filters and fan belts and I had every conceivable spare part tucked away in the bilge.

At about 9:35am I fired up the engines to let them warm up. They hummed responsively as they always did, but I knew that they wouldn't get a break for over twenty-three hours, and they had never been worked for that long before. Aidan and Dad untied us at 9:45am and, as the women waved goodbye and Paul filmed, we headed towards the entrance to Cork harbour and the Celtic Sea beyond.

Driftwood passed Roche's Point Lighthouse at 10am right on schedule. We rose and fell gently on the swells as we pointed the bow towards nothing at all. I still had a signal on my phone and managed to get through to Donal. A few minutes later Donal rang me back to tell me that the wind may reach a force four but it was still due to drop again in the evening. I thanked him and we forged on as land fell over the horizon behind us. In front of us and to either side there was nothing but water. The feeling was one of excitement and nerves. Eventually we could not see land at all - and a lot was to happen before we saw it again.

Each hour we took our position from the GPS and plotted it on a small scale chart. This was proving a bit disheartening because we had to move a total of about two feet on the chart and were progressing at the rate of about one inch an hour.

We sailed on a course of 137 degrees true rather than using the GPS to go to a waypoint. This was because the tide would pull us left and right over the time of our course as we would be travelling through almost four tides. The plan was that in the morning when we were about twenty miles from land we would use the GPS again and travel to a waypoint. This would reduce the amount of fighting against the tide to a minimum. Put simply, we needed to keep the compass needle pointing at the same point for the next twenty-four hours or so.

Eventually at about 2pm off to our right we could just make out the gas platform of the Kinsale Head Gas field. Here gas is taken from deep beneath the sea floor and then used to heat Irish homes and to cook Irish dinners. Not a nice place to work, I thought, a bit of a commute.

There was nothing to photograph but we photographed anyway just to pass the time. The day passed without incident and the sea state remained quite comfortable.

It was early evening at about 6pm when Aidan called "ship ahoy." A large container ship, the first vessel we had seen since we left Cork, appeared on the horizon off our starboard side and it looked like it would pass very close to us. But would it pass in front of us, behind us, or through us?

I put the radar on to track it and also to get a bit of experience because using this old outdated radar was completely alien to me. There is a thing on radars called an EBL. Those who are in the know are probably familiar with EBLs. I'm not, so I got out a book about how to use radar when you are in the middle of the Celtic Sea and a large container ship looks likely to want the same bit of sea as you do, and at the same time as you do. The book lifted the Electronic Bearing Line mystery and I tracked my first vessel on radar. Feeling very chuffed with my newfound skill I proudly informed Dad and Aidan of the result of the bearing test. "Yep, we're on a collision course with that container ship alright." When I later recalled the course of action we took to avoid a collision to a yachty in a pub in Newlyn he put his two hands over his face in an attempt to block out the mental image and said: "Oh NO…NO… NO...NO… You accelerated?…. ACCELERATED!!!… That's the worst thing you should do." "Yes," I said, "I realise that now, but we did miss it by quite a bit, well, relatively speaking anyhow."

It was a bit worrying at the time because we were so close that we couldn't see the ship's bridge windows any more, so I presume that he couldn't see us either. Although I think whoever was supposed to be on watch at the time had gone to the loo or gone to watch telly or gone to play a game of golf on the back deck because we tried to call him on the VHF and couldn't get any answer. We gradually got closer to the bow of this big ship, a big ship that was closing in by the second. We could see that it was a little closer than we had thought. We could clearly see the large bulb that ships of its size have just below the surface at the front of the boat. I pushed the throttles all the way forwards but we were already at full speed. The ship was wider than you would have guessed, and it was travelling much faster than you would guess too. It's not a good idea to guess. But eventually the far side of the vessel started to come into view and we knew we were out of its path, and a lot wiser too.

It was now just after six in the evening and the wind was due to drop. It had been blowing a force two to three, occasionally gusting to force four, but the forecast said it would be dropping back to a force two this evening and tonight. As yet there was no sign of it slackening; in fact it seemed to be getting a bit rougher.

Aidan made up a dinner of boiled rice and a few tins of chicken á la something. He had a job because the pots kept trying to ski to the floor and in the end he had to hold both pots until they were ready. Aidan had his food with Dad while I kept watch. I was becoming increasingly uneasy because the wind was increasing to a level where under normal circumstances I would never venture out at all. We were out of radio range with the Coastguard so we couldn't get an update of the forecast. I comforted myself that there was absolutely nothing I could do about it anyway so maybe ignorance was bliss?

When Aidan had finished his grub he took over on watch and I joined Dad while he finished his. My Dad is the slowest eater on the planet; most of what he eats has gone cold. Amoebas eat quicker.

We used damp tea towels on the table to stop the dinner from escaping from us in an attempt to avoid being eaten. I had a knot in my stomach by then and I had to force myself to eat. I knew that we had another fourteen hours to go before we made land and I would need something substantial in my stomach to see me through the night. I wasn't quite in the mood for sleep. As I ate I looked out the window. All I could see was an angry sky. I took another mouthful of dinner. It was hard to swallow. I looked out the window again and all I could see was an angry sea. "It's a bit rougher than I had hoped," I said to Dad. "It is, but the boat is well able for it," Dad replied. I know I thought, but am I, I wonder? I could sense the concern in his voice too and I knew he was putting up a brave front.

I made out a shift roster for the rest of the night. I planned it so that there were two of us on watch at all times and one resting. This meant a 'four hours on, and two hours off' rota. It allowed all of us to get some rest during the night.

I went back out to Aidan. There was nothing on the horizon in any direction. "The wind will probably drop at dusk," said Aidan. I later made a list of things you should never say on a boat: "The wind will probably drop at dusk" featured in that list, but not at the top. Dusk came and went and the wind didn't drop. The flag on the back of the boat was making a buzzing sound in the wind. At about that time Aidan said we were at the halfway point. Night was closing in and there were white caps on the waves in all directions. Real sailors say that a lot of white caps indicates a force five wind. We both felt apprehensive.

"Ninety miles from land in either direction," Aidan said. "No we're not." "We are...I checked it," said Aidan. "We're not, we're only ninety-eight meters from land," I said. "How did you come to that conclusion?" asked Aidan. "Have a look at the depth sounder." Black humour is probably an Irish thing.

I quoted an old friend of mine, Jimmy Bright, who famously announced in response to someone commenting on the windy conditions: "There was often more wind in my stomach." In Jimmy's case, this was probably true. It was becoming necessary to hold on tight with both hands. We were taking the waves on our port side and the boat was rolling a long way past the comfort point. Eventually I decided to alter course to port, to point us into the waves a bit and reduce the pitching. This, however, meant that we were no longer heading in the correct direction. It was Aidan who said that it was still uncomfortable, so "if we're going to be uncomfortable we might as well be pointed in the right direction." I had to agree so we went back on course again and once more took the waves broadside.

Aidan said: "At least the engines are running fine." It was this statement that was later to top my list of things you should never say on a boat. As soon as he had the words out and as the last remnants of the sun faded beneath the horizon, we were hit by a big wave. I stumbled and grabbed the dashboard to stop myself from falling. As I did the revs on the starboard engine fell off and I thought it was going to stop. I gave it more throttle and it picked up again. "Did you bang off the throttle?" Asked Aidan. "No." I said. "You must have." said Aidan. "Maybe I banged it when I stumbled," I said, but I knew that I hadn't. I knew that we had developed an engine problem in the starboard engine. The knot in my stomach grew.

It was a very dark night. Any light from the moon was blocked out by sinister clouds. We estimated that it would get bright at around 5am so we had about six hours of darkness ahead of us. Every now and then we would burst into tune, and sing 'For those in peril on the sea.' I don't mean that we sang the whole hymn, we just sang that line, and thankfully we didn't know any more of it.

I was concerned that it was becoming very difficult to get around inside the boat without falling or banging into something and if Dad fell and injured himself out here it would be a major problem. So I asked him if he wanted a lie down. "Well I would love an hour to close my eyes," he replied. Dad has the ability to catch some sleep even while all around him, people are high on adrenalin. Aidan and myself decided we would keep watch together all night and the roster was binned. It was a great relief to have him there with me that night.

There seemed to be plenty of traffic around. We could often see lights but only occasionally could we identify if they were trawlers or large ships because all the colours seem to merge in the distance so that they all appear as white lights.

I'm not sure what time it was when the starboard engine spluttered again. It was probably about 1am. This time though it did not recover with a bit of extra throttle, and it cut out completely despite my best efforts.

I looked at Aidan in disbelief. Here in the middle of the Celtic Sea in the middle of the night the starboard engine had stopped. Fear was starting to get a hold.

On *Driftwood* you have to start the engines from the inside steering position. So as soon as I had accepted the fact that one engine had let me down I immediately scrambled inside to turn the ignition key. To my surprise it started straight away. However, it was short-lived. About twenty minutes later it stopped again. I knew that it was a fuel problem. I knew it was not getting enough fuel. But I had fitted new fuel filters in Cork and even the ones I had taken out were spotless, so a blocked filter was ruled out. Bad fuel didn't explain it either because both engines had run fine for fourteen hours or more on the same fuel, without any problem. Anyway, it was only the starboard engine that was giving trouble.

Once again the engine started up for me but it took a while this time before I could get it going again. The sea had become decidedly uncomfortable by now. It was imperative to hold on at all times. We had taken down anything that was likely to roll around the place and put it in into cardboard boxes. Now the cardboard boxes were sliding around.

The dark night meant we seldom saw the waves coming and so the occasional large wave caught us off guard, and the boat would pitch violently. We kept two bottles of minerals outside with us because our mouths were constantly dry and now our hands were becoming sore from hours of gripping on tightly.

The rib was held on davits that hung off the back of the boat. I had criss-crossed tension straps to prevent the rib from rocking from side to side and wearing a hole in its side. However, now I could see that the davits themselves were bending left and right with the rolling of the boat. I tried to think of a plan of action in case one of the davits broke off. I still haven't come up with one.

Since we had set out before 10am that morning we had been marking up our position on the chart each hour. This helped to pass time for us, especially during the night.

We marked big events like a quarter of the way there or a third of the way and half the way and so on. It was at 3am that things got really bad. The starboard engine had cut out again and while I was trying to start it the worst possible thing that could have happened at that time, did happen: The port engine cut out too. Now both engines were dead, and we were adrift in the middle of a very rough Celtic Sea.

I decided that we should refuel so we grabbed the one-hundred-and-fifty litres I had kept in reserve from the bilge. Refuelling in the dark on a boat that is adrift and pitching badly is not easy. Aidan kept a hold of me by the scruff of my neck while I knelt on the side deck and with a large towel around the diesel cap to keep water out. I fitted in the pump and so we refuelled.

Dad had woken when the engines suddenly fell silent and all three of us must have looked like very worried people at that moment.

Once we had refuelled I went in and gingerly turned the ignition key with a few words of encouragement to old Betsy. Thankfully both engines fired up almost immediately and as we got moving again the boat became more stable. I expected the starboard engine to cut out after a few minutes but to my delight it didn't. We tried our best to analyse the symptoms. Refuelling definitely made a difference therefore a fuel leak seemed a probability at that time.

At around 5am we saw the distinctive flash pattern on the horizon. Two flashes every ten seconds. This was Longships lighthouse, and this meant that it was only about eleven miles away. The sky was getting lighter as dawn was about to break and, just as things seemed to be getting sorted, the starboard engine cut out again.

It had run fine for nearly two hours since we refuelled and now, with land just on the horizon, it was playing up again. Thankfully it started up straight away but this time it was short-lived. Within half an hour we decided we would have to go in just on the port engine. We were at the northern end of the Lands End Traffic Separation Scheme and it is not a good spot to break down. As Lands End drew closer the sea conditions deteriorated further. Just before 6am we rounded Lands End and turned north-easterly and headed for Mounts Bay and the port of Newlyn. "Do you pair want a cup of coffee?" Dad shouted up from the galley. "Oh yes please," came the unanimous reply. The course took us inside of Carn Rock. Sea conditions were quite rough with the mighty Lands End on our port side. Another ten minutes would see us into the lee of Mounts Bay then the rest would be plain sailing.

We decided to try to restart the starboard engine to give us some more speed and stability. It started straight away and we continued on.

Soon it was a fresh bright morning and the cliffs of Lands End made an awesome sight. Then the starboard engine stopped again. I tried to restart it but it refused to fire up. While I was trying to restart the starboard engine, disaster struck, and the port engine stopped too. I tried and tried but neither engine would start. We could see the calm water of Mounts Bay just ahead of us but we could not reach it. We were rolling violently and nothing would make either engine fire up. The large heavy solid wooden table was sliding around inside the cabin as though it were on ice, briefly I thought: "Jack was right, we should have screwed the bloody thing down with those three inch screws." The cardboard boxes had toppled over, spilling their contents, which were now thundering around the cabin floor. It looked like a scene from the film 'The Exorcist'.

In the middle of it Dad held on, wedged between the cooker and the seating. I kept trying to start the engines. Sometimes it felt like the boat was going to turn over.

I wondered: should I get everyone on deck and seal up the boat in case she flipped? If I did that then I would be increasing the likelihood of losing someone overboard, but I would also increase the chances of the boat surviving a capsize. I decided to leave everyone where they were, at least for the moment. I tried to start the engines again but they wouldn't even fire. I looked out the window. We had drifted too close to the marker on Carn Rock. That is it; the decision was made for me. I looked at the time, it was 6.10am. I scanned the sea all around me, but there were no other vessels in sight. With a very, very deep sense of disappointment I did the only thing that I could do. I picked up the VHF:

"Hello Falmouth Coastguard. This is motor yacht *Driftwood,* over." Almost immediately the coastguard replied.

"*Driftwood* go ahead, over."

"Falmouth coastguard we have a situation," I spoke slowly and clearly. "Our position is five zero, zero three, decimal four six north, zero five, four eight, decimal four niner west, about half a mile north east of Carn Rock. We have complete engine failure on both engines, three persons on board, over."
That was it, I couldn't take the words back now. I didn't want to anyway.

"OK, *Driftwood* stand by over."

A short pause ensued. Still bigger and bigger waves buffeted the boat. Then Falmouth coastguard came back on and looked for our drift speed and direction. "How the hell are you supposed to work out your drift speed?" I said. "It's on the GPS," said

Aidan. "See, one point nine knots, and eighty six degrees."
"Good on ya." I said. Then I got back on the radio and gave
them the details.

We were getting caught up in the rough water that surrounds
the submerged Carn Rock.

"*Driftwood,* this is Falmouth Coastguard over."

"Go ahead over."

"There are no vessels in your area and given the proximity to
Carn Rock we have tasked Sennen Cove lifeboat. They will
advise as soon as they launch, over."

The sense of failure was very real now. With the finish line in
sight too. I apologised to Aidan and Dad. "I thought I had
everything covered but I must have missed something with the
fuel supply." "We were just unlucky," said Dad. "I'm glad you
didn't wait any longer to call the Coastguard" said Aidan.

Dad was holding on in the galley while Aidan and myself were
sitting on the back deck by the helm. We were sitting flat on the
floor with our backside on the deck and our legs spread-eagled
out in front of us as we wrapped our arms around the railings
on the back deck. Standing up was not possible. Then a voice
said: "Do you still want that coffee?" Unbelievably, even in
these conditions, Dad was still holding the kettle over the gas
to try to make coffee. We thanked him and told him to cop
on and hold on! Time dragged on. This time we could see the
waves coming but it didn't make it any easier. Occasionally an

exceptionally large wave would appear out of nowhere and set a new pitch angle record.

"Hello *Driftwood* this is Sennen Cove Lifeboat, over."

I had to crawl to the VHF and then wedge myself into a safe corner to answer the call. As I did, I could see the Tyne class RNLI boat sending bursts of white water hurtling into the air as she sped towards us. Coxswain Terry George and his volunteer crew were a very welcome sight.

Initially they were going to try to put an engineer onboard but the conditions just didn't allow it. The lifeboat came about and was stationary off the port side. They decided to take us in tow. This meant that I had to make my way up to the bow to secure the tow rope. I started to climb along the starboard side just as a wave hit us and the boat heaved badly to starboard. I crouched down and held on as the gunnels were submerged beneath the wave. At that moment I was sure the boat would flip over on top of me, but it recovered. Terry thought I had gone into the water and so did Aidan. Terry gunned the lifeboat to bring it around to the starboard side to pick me up, only to see me emerge at the front deck still holding on, with a grip like a Scotsman on a £5 note.

The lifeboat came past the bow and, as she did so, a crew member threw a rope to me. The rope had a knot on the end called a monkeys fist, this acts as a weight to help when throwing it. I looked at the rope, which was about as strong as a child's skipping rope. For a brief moment I said to myself: "Are these guys really going to try to tow us with something this flimsy?" Then the penny dropped. This was to pull the much heavier tow rope on board. Once I had secured the rope the lifeboat started the tow, they let out about three hundred feet of rope - so much that the centre of it was constantly in the water. This helped to absorb the tugging on the line. Dad checked his watch. The time was 6:45am, just thirty-five minutes since we had first made the call to Falmouth Coastguard.

Within about ten minutes we were in the lee of the headland and at the mouth of Mounts Bay. The sense of relief all round was very real. Between the three of us we got a few bob together so that Terry could get his crew a few pints as way of a very inadequate thank you. We all settled in for the tow into harbour and we drank the coffee that Dad made.

The newfound calm was broken when Aidan dived across me, grabbed a two litre bottle of 7up and, started squirting it all over the inflatable dingy that was still hanging on the davits. "What the hell are you doing?" I asked. "I threw my cigarette butt away and it landed beside the petrol can in the inflatable." Can you imagine if it had gone up in flames? The first thing the life boat would have done would be to cut the rope.

We rang our respective partners, having first agreed to never mention the lifeboat, not so much because it would worry them, more because they wouldn't let us go any further if they found out. And so The Secret began.

Chapter Five

The problem with reptiles.

I T WAS JUST about 9am when we got tied up in Newlyn, twenty-three hours after we had left Cork. We climbed the ladder up the quayside and found it hard to walk because the ground kept wobbling. It was like walking on jelly that smelt of fish guts and diesel. We decided to go to the Seaman's Mission for a good breakfast. We brought our lifejackets so that everyone would know that we were seafarers too, and not just some old tourists that had just driven into town in a camper van. We had a great feed surrounded by tables of fishermen dressed in oil skins and woolly jumpers, who immediately knew that we weren't real seafarers because we had lifejackets.

Newlyn is a small picturesque Cornish town. Its narrow streets and laneways lead up steep hills and down the other side, while small windows peep out from the granite stone cottages that line the roadsides. Dad, Aidan, and I must have looked like a scene from *Last of the Summer Wine* when we walked around Newlyn.

I was flying the Irish tricolour off the back of the boat. This is perfectly acceptable so long as you fly the host nation's national flag on your mast. Now Union Jacks are not a big seller in Ireland. You could say that demand is quite slow. So I had no Union Jack with me and set about finding one before someone noticed the error of protocol. I went into a shop near the fish market that seemed to sell all sorts of interesting things. The man behind the counter was after having a long argument with the people from the Revenue and he vowed to never pay a penny of tax again. "They can close me down. Reckon I might as well just close the doors anyway. I only come here each day to get away from the wife." He was probably close to retiring age, but you could see that he had once been a well-built man.

"I want to buy a red duster, you know a Union Jack for a boat."
"What…" He leaned across the counter, his eyes assessing me as he spoke. "You won't get one around here and if you did you would be a brave man to fly it." His two hands were on the counter now and he was leaning closer. Spittle filled the air. I was tired and simple things confuse me when I'm tired so I just assumed that there was a simple explanation that eluded me right now, but all would come clear later. "I'm flying an Irish flag on the back of my boat and I don't want to cause any offence," I explained, "so I want to fly a red duster from the mast. That's the protocol."
"Well," he said "You certainly will cause offence if you fly that foreign Union Jack here. This isn't England you know? This is Cornwall."

"But you are English? Aren't you? "

"We're nothing of the kind. We hate the bloody English, we're Cornish and we have our own language too. Did you know that?" I didn't know that.

He opened a drawer beneath the counter and produced a small six-inch black flag with a white cross. It reminded me of the black flags that they flew in Ireland the time of the hunger strikers back in the early eighties, but I kept that memory to myself. "This is St Piran's flag. You should know that he was an Irishman." I didn't know that either. "We're all Celts, the Irish and the Cornish, not like those bloody Sassenachs up the road in England." I paid for the flag and went to leave but he cut me off by doing a quick duck-under-the-counter manoeuvre, and he was standing in front of the door to block my exit. It had been a while since he had a customer and he wasn't going to let this one get away so easily. He tried to interest me in some wellington boots, then a nice hat which didn't look so bad once he had blown the dust off it. It was when he took down two paintbrushes that I could take no more. At this point I crumbled and bought a packet of them saying that they will come in handy some day, and maybe they will. While he was counting the takings from the two transactions I made good my escape. I returned to the boat with the flag and paintbrushes. True to form there was not a single boat in the harbour that wasn't flying St Piran's flag. I was proud to hoist it up the mast.

Early that afternoon Foggy, Clegg, and Compo retired to a good pub, The Tolkern Inn, where we were to enjoy many a good meal, and a good Guinness too. But the best of all was the pork scratchings. You don't get pork scratchings in Ireland and it's a shame. They're little bits of a dead pig, his skin and fat mainly. They're lightly salted and baked in an oven, or else it's the other way round. They are the tastiest and best way to put your cholesterol levels into double figures in a single night. Wow, I miss pork scratchings.

There is an engineering shop in Newlyn. It's run by a guy called Dave. Dave has a few assistants, Chris, Col, and another Dave. Between them there is not much that they don't know about diesel engines. "Did you change your fuel filters?" "Yes," I said "It was the first thing I did." "And were they dirty?" "No they were very clean." "That's strange, you would expect them to be blocked or at least have some dirt in them." Said Dave.

The row of floating finger jetties in Newlyn is home to many small, brightly-coloured fishing boats. There were two or three yachts there too, but this is predominantly a fishing port. One of the yachts had a small white, windmill-type generator at the top of its mast. It made a good wind indicator for us, because it turned as the wind turns, always facing into it, and its propeller blades spun at a speed relative to the wind speed. That day its blades were spinning so fast it must have been generating enough electricity to run a small town. The RNLI station in Newlyn was also flying a flag on a tall flagstaff, and its flag too was held horizontal in the strong wind.

Over the few days we got to know quite a few people in Newlyn. John the fisherman didn't have a very high opinion of the EU. He was barred from bringing his boat into the Thames Estuary again because his last protest outside the Houses of Parliament was judged to have been somewhat excessive. He liked the Irish though, and he held an entry in the Guinness book of records, or at least he should, for the most words spoken in one sentence without stopping for air. John also liked to drink Guinness but he preferred to drink from a can, which is at least a venial sin in some parts of Ireland.

The Harbour Master in Newlyn was more than helpful and he let us use a floating finger jetty, which upset some of the fishermen. Some of them believe that they have rights on these jetties going back to Henry the VIII's reign.

By Sunday we had found a small and probably insignificant diesel leak. It was little more then a hint of a diesel leak at one of the fuel filters. We convinced ourselves that this was the cause of the starboard engine cutting out. The blades on the wind generator were still spinning like an old turboprop readying for takeoff.

"The wind will drop off at about 2am. Might slip out myself and do a bit of fishing." Jeremy owned a twenty-eight foot fishing boat and took full advantage of every opportunity to tell us: "These jetties were not built for pleasure boats, you know. Only supposed to be fishing boats here." We didn't want to upset the locals and I wanted to get moving again as soon as we could. A break in the weather, even in the middle of the night, could be enough to allow us to get around Lizard Point and make it into Falmouth. A check of the tide tables showed that the tide at the Lizards would turn at 3am. This would give a short window of slack water to round the mighty Lizard.

"Are you right?...Come on...are ye right?... I made you a cup of tea...come on, get up, it's 1am." Aidan dragged me out of bed and I got into my cold clothes. On looking out the window I saw those blades, still spinning as fast as ever. The RNLI flag told the same tale.

The three of us drank tea and coffee while the engines warmed up. It was difficult to manoeuvre the boat in the tight confines of the harbour with the strong wind hampering us. We slowly headed past the other finger jetties. Jeremy was nowhere to be seen, his boat remained silent at its jetty. I radioed the coastguard to inform them of our intended passage, so that someone ashore knew where we were. As we approached the harbour entrance the last few lights on the harbour wall bounced off the huge waves that rolled past the harbour mouth. They came from our right on their way to the shore, and as yet we were protected from their force.

As we exited the safety of the port the boat dropped down into a trough, then up, up, and up it went on a mighty wave. I gunned the engines and swung to the right to fight into them. I was driving both engines almost flat out because we needed every bit of horsepower we could get. Still we were only making six to seven knots. There is a cardinal marker about a mile-and-a-half outside the harbour and I knew we must pass to its left. At night it flashes a white light with its distinctive flash pattern and is easy to spot once you are not in a trough. The further out we got, the less shelter we had from Lands End off to our right. When we dropped down into the troughs we couldn't see the lights of the shore. Then the nose of the boat buried itself into the next wave as we climbed its face. We passed the cardinal marker and the Lizard got closer.

I looked at my watch. It was over an hour since we had left the comfort of the harbour. Still the wind blew and the radar confirmed that we were the only boat out there. The waves got bigger, and soon they got bigger again. "We have to turn around. This is only going to get worse," I said. We sealed the boat and all three of us held on at the helm. Turning in these conditions is quite dangerous. I contacted the coastguard to advise them that we were going to turn about and return to Newlyn. They noted our position and reminded us to report in as soon as we were tied up safely. "Right, here goes," I said. "Hold on tight." I spun the wheel to the left and gunned the right engine to full power. Then *Driftwood* followed. Broadside to these mountains of water, we fell down into a trough and, as we gripped on tightly, she pitched over to the left as she was powerless against the enormous wave that thundered beneath us. Eventually she came round and we were out of the worst. The wind and the waves then pushed us towards Newlyn again. Almost immediately the starboard engine died on us. I scrambled inside and turned the key, and soon she started again. "Just as well we didn't continue on to the Lizard," said Dad. We were disheartened that the engines were still not right, disappointed that the weather wasn't giving us any breaks and dejected because we felt like we were prisoners of Newlyn.

As we passed the cardinal marker again the waves were noticeably smaller. Then the lights of the harbour entrance came into view. We lined up, which meant going broadside again, but this time there wasn't any serious risk, then we headed into the safety of its walls. It was 3am when we tied up again at our finger jetty and I let the coastguard know all was well.

Aidan's time had run out and, with no sign of the engines getting sorted anytime soon, and the weather forecast still looking bad, he decided to call it a day and head back home. He was very disappointed that he didn't make it to France with us. I walked with him to catch the early morning train from Penzance to Portsmouth where he could fly home. "When you get on that plane Aidan, for God's sake, don't mention anything about the engines," I said. We laughed and then the train pulled out.

Meanwhile, in Mounts Bay Engineering the autopsy went on and on for hours, then hours became days. We tried a separate fuel supply and the engines still cut out. Eventually it was decided that the two fuel pumps must have failed at about the same time. A million-to-one event. So there was nothing else for it. The lads estimated about eight hundred pounds to have the two pumps reconditioned. "We will have it done for you in a week."

In the end it took two weeks and cost one thousand five hundred pounds, but that's boating for you. They say never buy a boat if you can't take a joke.

Myself and Dad decided that while the work was being done we would fly home and return as soon as the boat was ready. Before we left I sent a postcard to Donal in Cork.

The taxi pulled up outside the Seaman's Mission in Newlyn on the stroke of 7am, just as arranged the night before. A few minutes later we were in the train station in Penzance. The Pirate theme in the town can be credited to Gilbert & Sullivan rather than any great basis in truth. However, you should never let the truth get in the way of a good theme.

We got our tickets and waited on the train wondering, after boarding, whether or not we were on the right one. Before long it pulled out and we were on our way to Plymouth. The journey took a little over an hour and we pulled into Plymouth train station right on time. Here we took another taxi to the

airport a short distance away. Our flight was due to take off
at 11:25am and we were used to checking in two hours before
the departure time, but apparently if it's an internal EU flight
you only check in an hour before. The girl at the check-in desk
had one of those airline smiles and told us to come back in
an hour. She managed to say this without any change to her
facial expression at all; I think she was a glove puppet or an
android.

We headed to the café and had toasted cheese sandwiches
for breakfast. The menu in Plymouth Airport could never be
described as exhaustive.

An hour later they called our flight. We headed to the check-
in desk eagerly presenting our passports to the smiling airline
android. Still with the same smile she gave us our boarding
passes and in an "Oh I nearly forgot" type of way she told us
that our plane had technical difficulties and we were going
to be transferred by coach to Newquay where we would be
accommodated on another flight that would leave at 12:30.

"Is Newquay near Newlyn?" I asked, "Yes," said the android.
"We just came from Newlyn by two taxis and a train." The
android smiled in that "I don't' give a damn" kind of way. We
piled onto the bus along with forty or so other disgruntled
passengers. Still, these things happen. A little over an hour later
and we were nearly back where we had been when we woke up
at 6am that morning.

We headed into the airport just in time for our 12:30 flight.
A notice beside the queue told us we had to have a £5 airport
improvements ticket and that these were available from the
machine at the other end of the terminal. Dad headed over
and invested £10 in the Newquay Airport Improvement Fund.

Then we got to the check-in desk and the girl told us we didn't need to buy the ticket from the machine because we were transferred from Plymouth. Then we headed through security and into departures just as 12:30 approached.

Apparently we missed the announcement saying that the replacement flight was delayed but a girl told us that the flight would be boarding in about forty-five minutes. An hour later we were called to board. Ten minutes after that we were called to return to our seats again. We had to wait for a document to be faxed through. Ah, I thought, that will only take a few minutes. Two hours later one of those flat truck thingies came along and towed the plane away. The airline gave us vouchers for a cup of tea or a Cornish Pasty. The latter was a bad choice and to find out how old it was you would probably need to carbon date it.

Then, just before four, they announced that we would get on a flight to Dublin at 4:15. Then at 4:15 they announced that we wouldn't. Then they said they would fly us to Cork and bus us to Dublin but they didn't know when that flight would take off. I got my money back and they put us in a taxi and sent us back to Plymouth.

In Plymouth we went to the train station to see if we could catch a train to Exeter to make the 10pm flight to Dublin but we missed the train and decided to get something to eat because the toasted cheese sandwich had worn off by now. It was getting something to eat that caused us to miss the 7pm train too. The man behind the counter could see we were nearly broken men and suggested that we go to a pub called The Penny Come Quickly "It's the nearest pub. It's at the bottom of the hill." "Is Penny a girl?" I briefly pondered, then dismissed the thought.

In the pub we could unwind while we waited for the train at 9:15. By now we had realised that the 10pm flight was actually a 10am flight. Who cares? We will get a pint soon. When we got to the bottom of the hill we could see the pub ahead. When we got to the pub it looked like it had closed down about ten years ago, so we went back up the hill to the train station. A sign in the station lobby said: "This is an internet hot spot" but then the battery in my laptop went dead and my will to live began to slip.

When the train arrived we boarded and just then someone said that a bomb had gone off in Exeter and the whole town was under a security cordon. Being an Irishman in a strange town with no overnight bag and no good reason for being there, is not good. It's especially not good a few hours after a bomb has just gone off. It was probably the first bomb in Exeter since the Luftwaffe last paid a visit. It all made me feel more than just a little uncomfortable. It was 10:30 when we arrived into Exeter train station and we still had nowhere to stay for the night. A notice said that "We are on Red Alert." For some reason all of the public loos were locked. I don't know if this is standard policy in the event of a terrorist attack. Maybe the psychological profile people in the Anti-Terrorist Unit came up with the idea. "Yes sir, he will be dying for a pee. It's the smell of the Semtex, affects the bladder, so it does. Lock all the loos. Be ruthless about it. Sooner or later your suspect will have a distinctive wet patch. The weaker ones will just give themselves up."

There was quite a police presence at the station and all over the town. I heard that a man had been arrested at the scene of the explosion and I was keen to know what nationality he was. Was he a Muslim extremist or an Irish extremist?

We got a room in the Holiday Inn and it was the following morning when I saw an account of the day's events in a local paper. The bomber was named as Muhammad O'Reilly. What were the chances of that? Irish, Muslim, and extremist. Apparently he had a learning disability and had converted to the Muslim faith only a few weeks previously. That's when he changed his name to Muhammad. It didn't say, but presumably his name was originally Mick or Sean or something. I presume that the detailed psychological profiling had helped to crack the case.

We got on our flight at about 10am and were in Dublin a little over an hour later, nearly twenty four hours after our original flight was due to take off. It only took twenty three hours on *Driftwood*. We beat the aeronautical world by an hour!

"I have the pumps fitted and both engines are running like a dream." Dave is my hero, and his voice at the other end of the phone line brought the news that I had been waiting for. We had been back in Ireland for two weeks. I checked the weather forecast on the net and it looked good. Then I rang Dad and we booked our flights back to Cornwall.

When we arrived in Plymouth we went to a good ships chandlery, and I was able to buy all the charts I needed for the remainder of the sea passage.

Between the time we booked our flights and the time we actually arrived in Cornwall the weather had changed again.

There was a strong wind, about a force six, so we decided to wait and see what it would be like in the morning. Anyway a meal in the Tolkern Inn would go down well.

In the morning things weren't much better. I walked around the harbour talking to fishermen whenever they would talk to me. I quizzed each one about the Lizard. This is no reptilian monster but the most southerly headland in the UK (sorry I meant to say Cornwall) and a nasty piece of work it is too. Lands End has an almost unrivalled reputation for claiming boats and the lives of careless or unlucky seafarers. However, the locals say that Lizard Point has a similar if not a worse reputation.

Some say you must keep three miles off the head, others say anything less than five miles and you're being foolhardy and, of course, you must round it at slack water, preferably on a neap low, especially if you're heading east. Dragons live in the waters and they eat sailors for breakfast. Serpents ten times the size of your boat will thrash you into smithereens if they spot you. After all it's called the Lizard for a reason. It's worse than the Bermuda triangle. Even the Royal Navy give the Lizard a wide berth when they exit out of Plymouth. Watch the wind: An easterly is worst but so is a westerly and a southerly will send you into the shallows but a northerly is the worst of them all. Best to wait till there is no wind at all or put your boat on a trailer. Better still go by bus and save all the hassle.

On the morning of June 6 we headed out to round the Lizard Head. The wind was at about a force four, but we had been stuck for three weeks in Newlyn and I wanted to get moving again. We left two hours before high water so that we would arrive at the headland as the tide turned and take advantage of the short window created by this slack water. The engines purred and the swells lifted us high then dropped us down only to lift us up again. The sea was uncomfortable but we were moving again, getting closer and closer to our goal. It was when we were midway round the Lizard that the starboard engine cut out. I couldn't believe it. I rang David straight away and I think he thought that Satan himself was on the phone to him. "Can you make it into Falmouth?" he asked and I agreed that that's what we would do. When we got to Falmouth I was feeling very down. The engine problem was starting to beat me. It was my torturer slowly pulling out my fingernails and applying electric shocks to my nether regions.

The marina was very full because there was a boat rally from some yacht club and we had to double-moor. Now a twin-engine boat will do fine on just one engine except for one thing: it is almost impossible to moor up with one engine that is mounted on one side of the boat. By the third attempt the rally events had been put on hold to allow the participants return to their boats and protect them from the mad Irishmen who were spinning out of control in the marina. With lots of help from the ralliers we eventually got tied up and went to the pub for dinner. The pub advertised that they had an internet hot spot so I went back to the boat and got my laptop, but their hot spot wasn't working, so I had a beer and dreamt of a boat that had an engine that didn't break down.

The next morning Chris from Mounts Bay Engineering arrived. Well, he got lost first, and actually arrived at about lunch time. Chris has a very thorough and systematic way of thinking. First he went to the fuel tank and pulled off the fuel line.

Diesel spilled everywhere. "That's grand. We have diesel here," he exclaimed. He put that back together. Next he went to the lift pump and pulled off the fuel line there and, guess what? No diesel. Somewhere between these two points there was a blockage. We knew we were close to finding the cause of the engine failures. The main suspect was a water trap, a glass bowl thingy that is supposed to catch any water that may be in the diesel by allowing the heavier water to fall to the bottom of the glass bowl before it gets into the engine. "You changed the filter on that didn't you?" "Errr wot….there is no fuel filter on the water trap….. is there?" Of course there was a filter in the water trap, and of course it was blocked. It was the first filter on the line and I didn't even know it existed.

I had been changing the second and third filter on the line and, of course, they were clean because the dirt was collecting in the first filter. I should have been annoyed with myself, but I wasn't. I was delighted because this was our problem all along. We changed the filters on the water traps for each engine and both of them were blocked up completely. When we refuelled in the middle of the night out in the Celtic sea, the weight of the extra fuel in the tank helped to push the diesel through the blocked filters.

Now I had full confidence in the engines again. However, it was too late to head out so we went for a bite to eat instead. Later I refilled the jerry cans and the fuel tank in preparation for the trip in the morning.

June 7 was a Saturday, the sun was shining, the wind was force three, the engines were purring as if to say "Bout time you gave us some diesel" and the forecast was good for the next few days. We cast off and headed out of Falmouth and into the sea beyond. We followed the coast all day and it was a great feeling to be so confident of the engines again. We passed Plymouth keeping well off the shore. A Royal Navy warship cruised about the entrance to Plymouth Harbour as if it were protecting it from an imminent naval bombardment.

The Eddystone lighthouse was just visible on the horizon off our starboard side. The wind picked up as we approached Start Point and then the sky darkened, the clouds formed into a colossal dark doughnut in front of us, and suddenly dramatic bolts of lightning struck the water from the substantial thunder cloud above. We could see the rain pelting down from it but as yet it was still a mile or so in front of us, but heading for us. There were a number of yachts about and quickly they turned and made for Salcombe bay. We were further from shore and Salcombe was out of reach for us. If we ran for it we would find ourselves too close to shore when the storm would catch us. Better to keep out to sea, I thought, and ride it out.

We closed all the windows and secured the door so that the boat was sealed. Then we put on our waterproofs and adjusted our lifejackets to fit over them. The wind was against the tide so I was expecting the worst. The cloud looked awesome and soon we were alone as the last of the yachts slipped into Salcombe.

We held on tight as the storm approached. I wondered at our chances of being hit by one of the tremendous bolts of lightning that were striking the water ahead. Then a remarkable thing happened. As we started to pass beneath the cloud the wind changed direction completely. Now, instead of the wind coming from behind us, we were heading into it. This made a huge difference to the sea. Now we had the wind with tide and the sea fell calm again. We both laughed aloud with relief. We must have made ridiculous sight, standing out on the back deck in torrential rain and laughing noisily. The rain thundered down and we pushed on as around us bolts from the heavens struck the calm water.

It was probably about an hour later when we could see a blue patch of sky ahead and we knew that we would be out of the storm soon. As the storm passed behind us the rain stopped and once again the wind changed direction. The sun came out and we sailed between the two castles that protect the mouth of the Dart River. Dartmouth has to rate as the most picturesque town we came across on the south coast of England but they know it, and they charge accordingly.

We came to a mooring on our right and headed towards the long floating visitors' jetty with plenty of spare room on it. "You can't moor here, there is a rally coming here later." The woman on the jetty was tying up a yacht and barely looked at us as she spoke. "We don't want them here," she said to her friends with less discretion then she thought. "Where is the visitors' jetty?" I asked. "You can't moor here I told you." She was becoming impatient now. "I heard you the first time and second time. What I asked you was, where is the visitors' jetty?" I don't tolerate bad manners easily. "This is the visitors' jetty but we have it booked out so you can't stay here." She looked at her crew who stood there with their hands buried in their pockets up to their wrists and made nodding motions and shrugged their shoulders in agreement. She still didn't look in our direction. I wanted to explain to her that we weren't just sailors on some rally, we were explorers, we were on an adventure, we were on a mission, we were pushing out the boundaries, we were discovering new worlds. I wondered if Ernest Shackleton had the same trouble when he arrived at the South Pole. Did he have mooring problems because the south of England yachty brigade were on their way and had booked up all the available ice flows?

I conceded defeat and we moved on further up the Dart River past a beautiful three-masted sailing ship. We finally got mooring at Noss Marina. We tied up and I went up to the Harbour Master's office but there was no one there so I left a note and asked them to invoice me.

I returned to the boat to make a cup of tea. That's when Don emerged from beneath the water, like Neptune, only without the trident. He was clad in a diver's dry suit and clasping a length of stainless steel bar that apparently was a vital component of someone's canopy. We chatted for a while comparing old diving experiences. "Do you fancy a cup of tea?" I asked Don, "Oh yeah, I'd murder for one." "In that case you might take a quick look at my propellers, and make sure there isn't a piece of rope caught on them." Don obliged and we enjoyed a good chat over several mugs of tea. He told me all about his life and his family and a nicer bloke you wouldn't come across too often. When Don was all tead out he headed away to get out of the dry suit and have an overdue pee that would probably set a new Dartmouth record.

We decided to head up the town for a bit of bar grub. When you are looking for a lift it is important to play on other people's sympathies, so looking as bedraggled as we could we started walking along the roadway that leads out of the marina. We must have perfected the art because the first car to pass us stopped and reversed back. "Would you guys like a lift into town?" "That would be great, thanks very much." We jumped in, and a nice couple drove us into Dartmouth while we waxed about our adventures. The trip into town included a jaunt on the ferry across to the other side of the river. They dropped us off in the town centre and recommended a few pubs where we would get good food. We enjoyed what was really just a mediocre meal which we washed down with a pint. Later we returned to the marina by water taxi and settled in for the night.

In the English channel the tides show no mercy to anyone who doesn't take due regard of them. We got up early to make the most of the tide that would sweep us up along the coast of Lyme Bay and all the way to Weymouth. This was to be the last of the English legs. Soon we would cross the channel.

We refuelled from a barge on the river called *The Dartmouth Crusader.* I was surprised to see that the owner not only opened from 8am to 8pm seven days a week, he took credit cards too. We found that an awful lot of businesses in the UK do not take credit cards and prefer cash instead and that's a nuisance because there's not an over abundance of ATMs at sea.

We headed out past the sailing ship at 8:30am, and past the yachty rally as they slept, then out between the two castles, past The Mewstone rock. We could have taken a straight line across Lyme bay, a distance of about forty-five nautical miles, but it was a lovely day with no wind and we were in no hurry so we followed the coast where we had something to look at, even though this put about another thirteen miles onto the journey. We passed Torquay and I was reminded that this was where Basil Fawlty had his hotel, on past Exmouth and Lyme Regis.

We were cruising at about eight knots, the sun was shining, there was no wind and I knew that the engines would keep running without a bother for as long as I needed them to. This was idyllic cruising and we relaxed completely. But, then we got too relaxed.

The trip was in such perfect conditions that we decided to take time out to set the compass. Setting a compass is a task best left to an expert. But we didn't have one so we decided to have a go ourselves.

We had two types of compass on the boat. There was a GPS compass that will tell you the exact course the boat is travelling on, which is not always the same way that it is pointing, because wind and tide have an effect too. Then there is a plain old magnetic compass which tells you what direction you are pointing, but not necessarily which way you're heading, again because of tides and wind. Then there is another problem with the magnetic compass: it is affected by any metal objects around it. Now, given that *Driftwood* is a steel boat, the magnetic compass tends to be a bit unreliable.

Because the weather was fine, with no wind to affect our direction, and because it was now slack water, we decided to potter around in the lazy sunshine and see how the magnetic compass compared with the GPS compass at different headings. This meant travelling in a huge circle and recording lots of numbers and stuff. About an hour and a half later we had a sort of chart thing that sailors call a deviation chart. We needed this to cross the Channel.

Unfortunately the good weather had made us casual and I forgot one vital thing about boating in the English Channel - the tide. I had missed my chance to round the headland they call The Bill of Portland. Probably not very wisely, I decided to fight against the tide and round it anyway. After all there was no wind. As we neared the headland the current increased and our speed reduced. Eventually we were only making two-and-a-half to three knots against the current. The sea around the headland was very rough and even though there was no wind, there were white horses all across the surface as the sea tried to squeeze around this protruding headland. Off to our right was a sandbank called The Shambles, which funnels the water further and the trip was at a snails pace. It took well over two hours to cover the seven miles that brought us to Weymouth.

As we approached the harbour *The Normandy Express,* a high speed ferry, approached from behind us. We moved to one side to give her right of way. She went ahead of us into the harbour and we kept close to the harbour wall so as to keep out of her way. I have since noticed that fishermen don't like it when you do that. It tends to costs them a lot of tackle. Ah well…

I radioed the Harbour Master to see if there was a mooring and he told me to raft up on the visitors' jetty. We approached the jetty, where most boats were double-moored. There was a steel yacht, probably a forty footer with no one rafted outside it, so we latched on. Priscilla, the owner, had sailed it singlehanded from Canada and now she was circumnavigating the UK. It was a big boat and she must have been a very skilled sailor to do it alone. We felt like a pair of sissies beside her.

Weymouth is one of those old English seaside resorts. The seafront has colourful beach huts, candyfloss stands and shops selling plastic buckets and spades.
There are also sand sculptures. These are protected with three-quarter sheds and chicken wire to prevent vandals reducing all

the hard work to sand. We didn't have time to explore so we went back to the boat and got down to business.

We dug out charts because we had a lot of work to do in preparation for tomorrow's voyage across the channel. The tide was going to be a huge factor. I drew lines on charts and then I drew tidal vectors, and I checked books and then I drew more lines and then more vectors. I drew estimates of our position each hour and plotted our course.

The plan was to head out in the morning and go around The Shambles to the East Cardinal Marker that marks the eastern end of this sand bank. That's about one hour's cruising time from Weymouth. We needed to pass this marker at 11:30am then hold our magnetic course of 155 degrees for about another seven hours. This way the strong tidal currents around the Cherbourg peninsula would work behind us and push us into our intended port of Omonville. This was the sort of navigating I had only done in a classroom before, so we were taking a bit of a chance.

We had to shelve plans to go to Cherbourg because the French fishermen were blockading the ports in protest at high diesel prices, so we decided on Omonville instead. When the plan was agreed we went in search of bar food, which was a longer search than expected. We did eventually get grub but some Brits haven't got a clue about pouring Guinness. Unlike ale or lager, pouring a Guinness is an art form. It cannot be rushed, and must be allowed to settle before you add the final quarter. After a chat with the helpful barman he pulled a superb pint of Guinness and we enjoyed a pleasant evening before returning to the boat.

In the morning I fired up the engines and they purred enthusiastically. I decided to top up with diesel, not because I was worried we would run out but more because the French fishermen had a point - diesel was about €1.50 a litre in France at that time.

There is an inner harbour in Weymouth and access is restricted by a lifting bridge. Just as I untied, the bridge lifted and half the boats inside headed out and half of them wanted diesel so we ended up last in the queue.

With both tanks full *Driftwood* holds 750 litres and with the jerry cans in the bilge filled too, we had another 150 litres in reserve. This gave us a theoretical range of about sixty hours.

We eventually got filled up and at 10:35am headed out of the harbour. The anglers all hauled in their gear when they saw us coming.

Chapter Six

Ooh la la, it's the Channel

WE HEADED OUT of the bay and as we did so Portland Coastguard announced a Pan Pan Call. A Pan Pan is one step down from a Mayday. It normally means that a boat is broken down but there is no immediate risk to life.

We plotted the position of the casualty, a small fishing boat, who could not get his engine to start. He was about an hour and a half away so we weren't much use to him. I was glad anyway because timing is vital in this crossing and any delay would mean that we would have to return and try again when we had recalculated the tides.

The Royal Naval war ship *The Tyne* answered the call and launched a rib with a mechanic on board to get him going again. Once the Pan Pan was stood down I contacted Portland coastguard to tell them our destination and the time we expected to arrive in France. "Is that boat registered with the

Coastguard?" came the reply. I had to think, then I said: "No we are a visiting vessel from Ireland." that should keep him quiet I thought, but not so. The English are a very exacting race. "What is your MMSI number?" I gave him the number and he still wanted more. "What port are you registered with?" Now here is this registration thing again. God, they just keep at it don't they? "We're registered to Drumsna on the River Shannon." I reckoned that by the time he finds Drumsna on a map we will be well out of British waters. "Can you spell that for me?" I spelled it out. There was a long pause. Then Portland Coastguard came back on. "Er *Driftwood*..... have a safe passage.... Out."

We kept The Shambles sand bank on our starboard side and arrived at the East Cardinal Marker at 11:35am just as planned. Seven more hours and we should be in France.

The weather was super-calm, although a little misty. The current in the channel is incredibly strong. You are not aware of it until you come across a reference point, the likes of a lobster pot marker. Even though these markers were the size of beach balls they were often held below the surface by the racing current. We continued on and plotted our position each hour as we had done before when crossing the Celtic sea. It was beginning to look like the estimated positions for each hour that we had plotted the night before were spot-on. I was very proud of the fact because it meant that we had managed to calculate all the variables correctly, but I wouldn't like to do it a second time, we're just not that lucky.

We came to the first shipping lane at 2:30pm and the traffic came from our port side. Huge ships, many times our size and all packed high with containers, trundled down the channel at well over double our speed. I thought it would be like trying to cross a motorway while towing a few sacks of potatoes, but it wasn't. There was a good distance between each ship and it was a simple matter of playing a giant game of chicken. If you just missed this one you would probably get across before the next one gets you. It took about forty-five minutes to cross the first lane, then there was a sort of imaginary central median that takes about another forty-five minutes. About halfway across the Channel we took down the red duster and the Cornish flag and I hoisted the French tricolour. Then we entered the traffic lane heading north-east. Another game of chicken and we were through it.

There was still no sign of land, the weather was holding and there was little or no wind. We pushed on and at about 5:30pm we saw our first sight of the French coast.

There was a mist on the surface of the water and this made identifying a feature on the shore that was also represented on the map almost impossible. The cruising guide said to keep about a mile offshore then line up the church steeple with the lattice beacon on the shore. The only thing was we could not see the shoreline because of the mist. We couldn't see where the land met the sea, and so we couldn't see either the church steeple or the lattice beacon. So we cheated and used the GPS. We picked a suitable waypoint that would be on the transit with the church and the beacon and headed to it.

We headed to this waypoint and, once there, we turned to 257 degrees as the cruising guide stated and headed straight towards the mouth of Omonville Harbour, which appeared out of the mist on our final approach. Dad and myself had got the phrase book out and the English/French dictionary. We had to contact Cherbourg coastguard to tell them of our safe arrival. "Bon jour Cherbourg Coastguard, je suis bateau nom *Driftwood*, je suis arriver Omonville pas danger, over." I was much chuffed at my first attempt at French. Then the radio crackled in response. "Hello *Driftwood* this is Cherbourg Coastguard. Thank you for trying to speak French, but we will do this in English."

It was 6:35pm, just eight hours after we had left Weymouth. We tied onto a large white triangular mooring buoy and launched the rib. A few minutes later we stepped off onto French soil. I put my hand in my pocket and took out my phone and wrote a text message. It simply said: "The horse has arrived safely in France." it was Monday June 9, 2008.

*   *   *

We tied up the rib and walked the short distance to the Bela Restaurant on the waterfront. Omonville is a picturesque small fishing town, with just one small shop, and so we felt quite lucky to find a restaurant. There we had mussels and chips and wine and beer. The chips were good but they must have gone fishing for the mussels at lunchtime. Well lunchtime for the mussels that is. Apparently mussels eat small soft-shell-crabs and almost every mussel had a small crab inside it which was nearly as distasteful for me as it must have been for the crab. Still, I never enjoyed a beer since as much as I enjoyed that first one in France and I've tried a few.

We returned to the boat and sat out to watch a beautiful sunset over the Channel. I went to bed very content that night.

At about 3:30am I awoke to the sound of the boat hitting something. Suddenly I could picture the boat aground on rocks after having parted from the mooring buoy. I jumped out of bed, threw on some clothes and grabbed a torch. As soon as I got on deck it was clear that we hadn't drifted at all. But then we banged something again. It was the large white pyramid-style mooring buoy having an argument with the front of the boat. No damage was done and I went back to bed. Needless to say Dad, who slept in the front cabin right beside the source of all the noise, slept through. So much for life at the sharp end.

In the morning I rowed ashore again, armed with a few euro, and headed up to the local shop. I was looking for sugar, some stamps, a postcard and toilet paper. I ended up getting two envelopes, no stamps, a box of sugar lumps and two litres of UHT milk. UHT milk is similar to real milk in that they both share the same colour. There the similarity ends. It's more nutritionally fulfilling to drink white emulsion paint. I have now learnt that you can mime most products that you want to buy in a shop if your French is not up to the job. I say most products: there is one product that you cannot or must not mime. If you try to mime 'toilet paper' it causes great offence as well as confusion and could easily end up in the courts if you're not careful. We will have to make do with our meagre stock.

I returned to the boat and we had breakfast. There was no hurry because we had to wait for the tide to turn so that it would push us east along the north French coast. We planned to go as far as Ouistreham before nightfall and we were getting impatient. We wanted more adventure, we wanted to feel the waves lift the boat and to hear white water at the bow as we plough our way along the French coast. And so we fired up the engines and nosed *Driftwood* into the approaching tide and managed a slow four knots against its flow. Still, four knots is faster than staying tied to a mooring buoy. We bade farewell to Omonville as she slipped into the distance behind us. Sod them, they can keep their toilet paper.

As Omonville disappeared the great port of Cherbourg came into view on our right. There was a lot of traffic on the radio but we couldn't understand it as it was all in French. Then a French naval ship came into view between us and Cherbourg, then another one and then a third one. Wonder is there a naval exercise going on? I thought.

They were lurking about. On the radio the Coastguard kept repeating the same message and each time they gave the same grid reference. We plotted it on the chart even though we didn't know why we were plotting it. It was a spot in the sea between us and the shore. We had the feeling that everyone else knew something that we didn't know. The navy were still lurking. The coastguard was still talking and we were still scratching our heads and plodding along. Then the guy in the coastguard who can speak English came on the radio and told us that there was going to be an underwater explosion at 11am, and he gave the same location that had been repeated several times before.

As 11am approached we poised with cameras, video cameras and mobile phones at the ready. Then the radio sparked into life, *dix, neuf, huit, sept, six, cinq, quater, trios, deux, un...* And our cameras recorded the sight of nothing happening. A few minutes later it started again: *dix, neuf, huit, sept, six, cinq, quater, trios, deux, un...*

and again nothing happened. We were past Cherbourg now and getting further away from the potential explosion. Then Dad shouts: "Look, look." He is pointing towards the shore. "What?...I can't see anything." "Look, here it comes; it's heading straight for us," said Dad. I still couldn't see anything at first, then I saw it. It was low in the sky and had blended in with the land in the background. It headed straight at us. It was too late to grab a camera as the Dauphin Helicopter from the French Navy thundered over us, just a few metres above our radar mast, then it swung away again. We waited with our cameras ready for its return but, like the underwater explosion, we could still be waiting.

We passed Barfleur Point, the only headland that we would have to face on the French coast. My memories of cutting it close to The Bill of Portland were still vivid in my mind so I held a course that kept us well out to sea. Once safely round the headland I swung close to shore again.

Here the mood on board tempered. As the coastline came clearly into view so did Utah beach. I am looking at the same coastline that so many young men, many of them less than half my age, saw shortly before they faced the machine guns from the German defences on the beach. The mood became more and more sombre. I began questioning why so many men gave their lives close to this spot. Was it so that I could cruise by, years later, in luxury?

We headed past Omaha beach and further east along the coast. We were close to Arromanches and the Mulberry Harbour, built to ship in supplies to the allied troops who were driving the German forces from France.

I decided that we would try to anchor in the remains of the
harbour and half mast the flag. Then row ashore in the rib and
set foot on the shore here where so many young men had first
set foot on French soil.

As the harbour came into view so did another sight that I
had not expected to see. Speed boats, jet skis, families out on
fishing trips. As jet skis raced each other and dodged the speed
boats we approached the harbour entrance. The entrance is a
bit confusing. There is one red marker and a green one too,
but between them there is an obstruction in the water. The
guide book says not to drop your anchor because you will
probably never see it again; such is the amount of debris on
the bottom.

At the last minute I throttled back and pulled away from the
harbour entrance. I didn't want to add *Driftwood* to the debris
and I was unsure of the tidal height. I suspected that the tide
was too low for us to pass over the remains of whatever was
obstructing the mouth of the harbour. Out among the speed
boats again we promised to visit this site at the first opportunity,
and pay homage to those brave men.

We headed on past Gold, then Juno, and finally Sword. Here
we followed the line of markers that lead into Ouistreham. It
had been another long day - it was nine hours since we had left
Omonville that morning.

Ouistreham harbour is dominated by a tall lighthouse that can
be seen from well out to sea. Near the ferry terminal used by
Brittany Ferries there is a visitors' jetty but the maximum stay
is seven hours. There is also a large marina if you go through

the lock so that is what we did. The lock is dissected by a swing bridge and is large enough to hold a small ship. There is a second lock that is even larger; they built it just in case an aircraft carrier ever visits.

Once through the lock and into the marina, I viewed the visitors' berth. Every boat seemed to be double-moored, but then I spotted one that wasn't. Ah we'll tie onto him, I thought, and he is flying a red duster as all UK-registered boats do, so it's someone to talk to as well. "Do you mind if we tie alongside you?" I asked. The skipper was wearing a navy blazer with shiny brass buttons. This is a sure sign of plonkerism. "Well we are actually moving out early in the morning, at 7am," came the reply. I don't believe it, is he part of the south of England yachty brigade? This time there was only one of them so I wasn't going to be beaten. "That's no problem, I'll be up and I will move out to let you go." I had caught Plonker just before he disappeared into the cabin. I'm sure he thought about pretending he couldn't hear me but then thought better of it. "Alright so," came the reply and then he disappeared inside before I could throw him a rope.

We tied alongside. The skipper on another boat announced to the marina that he was going to go to the toilet. "You will need the code," said Plonker from the doorway, "It's 1953," he announced. "The year of the queen's coronation," he said, as he looked at me through the corner of his eye. "Is that right?" I said. "Same year Gerry Adams was born." I have no idea when Gerry Adams was born and I have probably just insulted him and, given his connections, that's not a good idea. Hey Gerry, if you ever read this, I didn't mean to insult you!

We headed out to a café for a beer and something to eat. The French have some strange customs. It's the practice here to kiss family and close friends on the cheek when greeting each other. They are also very animal-friendly. It's not unusual to see dogs being fed at the table in restaurants. In this restaurant the owner was kissing her dog just prior to greeting her close friends. A sign on the wall said no children after 7pm, I looked at my watch and it was 10:10pm. Evidently the ban didn't extend to doggies.

A beer or two later we waddled back to the boat, trundled across Plonker's boat as quietly as we could and went to bed.

At 6:30 in the morning I got up and Dad got up too. We waited for Plonker to get up but he didn't. 7am came and went and there was no sign of life onboard our neighbour's boat. I thought about waking him but then decided that letting him miss the tide would be a more fitting punishment. I got that one wrong. At 8am Plonker appeared and fired up his engine. "Can you untie? I need to catch the 7am lock." "I've bad news for you, you missed it. It's 8am now." Plonker checked his watch and said: "No it's only 7am." The debate about the time went on until Plonker announced that he was talking about British time. "But this isn't Britain," I said, "This is France." "Oh we always use British time," said Plonker. We let him out and then moored in the spot he had vacated. We never saw him again.

While some of the yachts were venturing out, we decided to stay put. The wind was up again and anyway we wanted to visit Arromanches to see the Mulberry Harbour and we felt we were due a bit of a break. We pondered if hiring a car was a good option and it probably would have been, but we got a taxi that cost €50 each way instead. Still it was worth it. We did the tours and lived each moment. It is a humbling experience to see what an incredible sacrifice that generation made, for our generation, and all future generations.

Afterwards we returned to a café in Ouistreham, where we had a beer and grub then mused through the bags of brochures we had accumulated. After another beer we returned to the boat.

The next morning I woke early after the sound of wind had disturbed my slumber. I got up and walked the short distance to the swing bridge that crossed the lock. From here you could see straight out into the channel to the open sea. The sight before me was worse than I expected. White foam covered the surface of the water. Weather forecasts in English are hard to come by in northern France, especially when you don't have a television. I didn't need one today, the scene before my eyes was clearer than any forecast. I closed my jacket against the wind and wandered up toward the town centre. Ouistreham is a clean, modern and slightly cosmopolitan town. There are several pedestrianised streets, with an abundance of cafés. Here people eat alfresco when weather permits. But more importantly there is an internet café.

A trawl of internet weather sites did nothing to cheer me up. A low system was closing in from the west and the outlook was for strong winds and unsettled weather for the next week at least.

I returned to the boat and Dad was up and had made a pot of tea. In the marina the boat is sheltered from the worst of the wind but even there it is obvious that we are going nowhere today. I told Dad about the forecast and the white surface on the channel and we drank tea and looked at charts and wind directions and drank more tea and did calculations and drew lines on the charts and then rubbed them out and drew more lines, then we drank more tea.

Our plan was to continue along the French coast as far as St Valery Sur Somme where we would enter the river Somme and thus the canal system. However, this was at least two more days along the coast and probably even a third day, as entering St Valery Sur Somme is a difficult task. Mud flats lie in wait to ensnarl pleasure boats and entering at the right time of the tide is essential. There was no sign of us being able to move for another week, so we looked at alternatives.

Le Havre and the river Seine were a lot closer. We could make it in about six hours from Ouistreham and from then on we wouldn't be held hostage by the weather. But we didn't have six hours of calm weather to get to Le Havre either.

Meanwhile, at home the 'other halves' were getting restless, news of another week-long wait didn't go down well either and all husbands know that: "Well… just do whatever you want," does not mean what we would like it to mean. So we decided to leave the boat in Ouistreham and fly home for peace talks. Unfortunately Dad had other commitments and he would not be able to come back out in the near future. But he had got the boat all the way from The River Shannon as far as The Canal De Caen in France. That's about 700 nautical miles, which is equal to about 800 statute miles, or 2,000 cups of tea and about six gallons of Guinness and probably twenty pub-grub dinners.

In the morning we got on the bus with our bags and headed to Paris, where we flew back to Dublin. The date was Thursday, June 12 and it was five weeks since we had left Kilrush Marina on the Shannon estuary.

Chapter Seven

Three wheels on my wagon

A FULL THREE WEEKS passed, and on Monday June 30 Marion and I drove the car onto the ferry at Dublin Port bound for Holyhead in Wales. The weather was typical Irish summer weather - wet, windy and cold. Once the car was stowed away we headed up to the main lounge where, with a coffee and a sandwich, we settled in for the three-hour crossing.

The plan was to drive across the UK from Holyhead to Portsmouth and then catch the ferry to Ouistreham where *Driftwood* was waiting.

We found a comfortable seat in the lounge at the bow of the ship. "Howya boss?" The enquiry came from a man in a well-worn suit. I guessed he was about fifty years old, was having a bad hair day and his unfortunate teeth-to-gum ratio was not helped by a few noticeable absentees in the front row. He was supping a pint of Guinness as he spoke. "I'm fine, how about you?" I said. "I'm grand, my name is Patrick." He held out a hand that you could paddle the ferry with if the engines packed in. "I'm Harry, glad to meet you." I said. "Don't like these boats ye know, don't like em at all. Will ye have a pint with me?" He asked. I declined, explaining that I never usually drink before breakfast. "I don't ate, all the goodness ye need is in that." He nodded towards the pint of Guinness, which was getting low now. "Will ye stick on another one there," he shouts at the barman. "Are ye sure ye won't join me?" "No thanks," I said. Mar was shuffling along the seat now to create some distance. "Did you mean that about not eating?" I asked. "Yeh, I never ates, ask me boy James Patrick… James Patrick comeer… comeer willya James Patrick before I have to go en get ye." James Patrick appeared. "Does I ever ate?" he asked James Patrick. "No he doesn't, never ates so he doesn't," says James Patrick. Then Patrick butts in: "Me father's name is James and he wanted the lad called after him, but I wants him named after me, so we sorta came to an agreement, that's why he's called James Patrick." He didn't say if the loss of his front teeth had any bearing on the matter. "What's bringing you to England?" I asked. "Lives there, normally lives around Nottingham but I goes wherever the work is. I'm a Traveller ye see." "I thought you were, alright," I said. "Loves travelling so I does, if I wants to go there, there's where I goes and that is that. I goes where the work is." "What sort of work do you do?" I asked. "Tarmacin of all sorts, mainly driveways. James Patrick goes ahead and finds the work and then me and me brothers come along and do the work. James Patrick is good at finding work." James Patrick was good at spending money too and he returned to get a second fifty euro note off his father. "The wife is at the other end of the boat. She doesn't like being near me on these boats, she's a bit nervous. One of these sank near Holland did ye know that? They forgot to close the door ye know. Wouldn't have liked to be on that one. Will ye stick on a pint there, will ya." Patrick was booking the pints at about the one-third empty mark to allow time for the fresh one to settle and still have a bit of an overlap.

We arrived into Holyhead right on time and I bade farewell to Patrick just at the same time his wife found him and, pulling him by the sleeve of his jacket, she dragged him towards the car deck.

The drive ahead of us would take most of the day and then we planned to board the 11pm ferry from Portsmouth to Ouistreham. The ferry would arrive into port at 6am on July 1. This was very poignant because at 6am on July 1, 1916 a lot of young men ate their last breakfast while waiting for the whistles to blow to signal to them to go over the top, in the bloodiest day in the history of the British Army. A great many Irishmen from north and south met their death on that day too, the first day in what became known as the Battle of the Somme. My own grandfather fought in that war and thankfully he came home after it, but so many more did not. What a lucky generation we were born into.

We sped along the motorway on our way to Portsmouth, and happily looking forward to six weeks on the French canals. All that remained was to move the boat along the coast to Le Havre. We decided to enter the river Seine at Le Havre near Honfleur as this would be quicker than going all the way to St Valery Sur Somme.

But then, just as we got close to Birmingham, there was a wobble. "Maybe I imagined that," I thought. But then there was another wobble. "Have I a puncture?" I thought so we pulled into the hard shoulder to check. A quick inspection showed that all tyres were fine so we headed away again. Oops there's a definite wobble, and then the car did a bit of a fish tail. I managed to get into the hard shoulder without taking anyone else with me. This time a quick look around and I diagnosed that a wheel had fallen off. Now with the notable exception of a Robin Reliant most if not all cars should have four wheels. But our one had just three with the forth only hanging on by a thread. Unfortunately it wasn't just loose wheel nuts. As soon as I went to tighten them I realised that the whole wheel hub was about to fall off the back axle. There was nothing for it so I rang the AA. "Are you a member sir?" The female voice at the other end of the line asked. "I am but I think my membership has lapsed a while ago." "Not to worry sir." She typed my name into her computer but the computer gave nothing in return. "When did your membership lapse sir?" She asked. "I think it was about seven years ago." I said.

After my credit card took a hammering they promised to have a truck out in an hour. Two hours later it arrived. It didn't take the AA man long to realise that this wasn't a job that you could sort out on the roadside. The car was hauled onto the back of the truck and we headed into Birmingham. At a garage they hoisted my car up on one of those hydraulic thingy's. Just about everyone employed in the garage stood watching as the hoist started to take the weight of the car. Then as the wheels left the ground the loose wheel fell off and landed at the feet of the mechanic. It was an embarrassing moment. Back in the office they did sums and rang suppliers. Then the man punched some numbers into a calculator and turned it around so that I could read it. They do that when they are afraid so say the figure out loud. "Is that a part number?" I asked. "No that's what you will owe us, and it will be lunchtime tomorrow before it's ready." I produced my credit card which was still wincing in pain after the AA incident. He stuck it in a machine and I think I heard it cry out.

I rang the ferry company and they were very nice about postponing our booking by twenty-four hours. Then we started the hunt for cheap accommodation.

Someone suggested the Etap Hotel in Birmingham City centre and just around the corner from the garage. Now Etap are certainly cheap, however there is a 'but'. If you are claustrophobic or if you would like your room to be more than just a little bigger than the bed that it holds then Etap is not the place for you. That said, it is basic and it suited our needs, even though we were the only people in the hotel who had English as our first language. After a shower to wash all the bad luck off us we went out for a well earned pint. We found a nice spot although it was a little quiet - there was just Marion, myself and the barman. He explained that this is a gay bar, even though he was the only gay person in it and he was heterosexually outnumbered by a ratio of two to one. I have no problem with gay pubs so we stayed for a few pints. After a few more pints we renamed the pub *The Cock Inn,* then left. Then we found that we were in what they call the gay village, more like a gay city as it's far too big to be called a village. Still, we enjoyed another pint and a meal before returning to the cupboard in the hotel where we slept.

The next morning started badly, I lay in bed and tried to remember how many pints of Guinness I had drunk the night before and when I remembered I tried to forget again. Then I dragged myself out of bed, took one step forward and walked into a wall. There was scarcely enough room to get dressed. My head hurt and my mouth felt like it was lined with Velcro, so I went downstairs and had some tea and orange juice. It was too early to attempt any solid foods. You could tell that this wasn't going to be a great day. I looked at my watch; it was 6:40am. They have just gone over the top I thought, the war to end all wars?

I went back to bed to see if I could sleep off the sore head. Later on I felt better and we got up and went to the Bullring market where you can buy anything for half the price you would pay elsewhere.

At lunchtime we collected the car and got under way again. We arrived in Portsmouth five hours early for the ferry because I was worried that we would miss it. It takes at least fifteen hours for five hours to pass when you're sitting in a car looking at a ferry terminal. As darkness fell they let us board.

Brittany Ferries are top class, the staff all wears smart uniforms and they are very helpful. Four of them at different times helped us find our cabin, which appeared to be large compared to the previous night's accommodation. We bunked down and the ship sailed across flat calm seas on its way to Ouistreham. They wake you very early in the morning with gentle classical music. This morning it was Barcarole, which was quite pleasant. If you didn't find it so pleasant you would need a Philips screwdriver and wire cutters in order to turn it off. I was clean out of both so we got up and went for breakfast at the sharp end of the ship. There we could see Ouistreham Harbour and the tall lighthouse ahead of us. The ship navigated the channel into port with ease and then managed a full 180-degree turn in the tight confines of the harbour before berthing. We made our way down to the car deck and found our car among hundreds of better ones. There we sat waiting for the ship's doors to open. Everyone else was doing the same, hoping that their row would be first off. Our row was last off because someone forgot to return to their car and we all had to wait for him. Still I think, of all the cars on the ferry, we had the shortest drive. We only had to go about a mile and a half, and then drive across the lock gates on the big 'Aircraft Carrier' lock and then across the swing bridge and the Marina just appears on the right hand side. And there she was… *Driftwood*.

Marion hadn't seen her since that day in Cork. We couldn't wait to get on board and make sure everything was ok, and everything was ok, just as Dad and myself had left it. "I never doubted that you had got it to France," said Mar. "But it just seems so strange seeing it here, so far from home."

Chapter Eight

On our last leg

MY PHONE BLEEPED in the familiar fashion to tell me that I had another text message. "We're at the front of the station," it read. I left the car parked in a very irresponsible manner and ran around to the front of the train station. There they were, my sister Ann and her partner Barry, our crew for the next leg of the journey. We drove the eight miles from Caen to Ouistreham where the boat was still moored. I told them about the wheel on the car and that we had only got here yesterday. We opened a bottle of wine and John and Eileen, who were on a yacht tied outside us, joined us for a few. Although they were both English, John and Eileen both loved Irish music and John loved playing it on his banjo. A fabulous and long evening followed.

It was about 9pm when Marion first noticed the rats. Then was more of them: they seemed to come out in the evening. All along the shore hundreds of rats ran about. Thankfully there didn't seem to be any on the floating jetties although I could see no reason why not. It gave us the shivers and all evening the music and craíc was interrupted by shouts of: "Would you look at the size of that one." Eileen found them especially repulsive and I failed to resist the temptation to wind her up. Occasionally I would run up along the deck with my hands down low as though I was trying to sweep them off the deck. At the same time I'd say "shoo shoo" and instinctively Eileen would have a panic attack and try to curl into a ball on the top of her chair. It worked best when I pretended to herd them onto her boat, saying: "Off the Irish boat, go on, get on the British boat."

I slept well knowing that Eileen was on rat watch most of the night. The following morning was Friday; the weather forecast gave us a twenty-four hour window when the wind would be down so we fired up the engines. The plan was for Mar to drive the car to Honfleur while Ann, Barry, and myself would take the boat along the coast and meet her there about six hours later. We entered the lock at the entrance to Ouistreham marina. There were a number of other boats there along with us, including John & Eileen's who gave me a few last minute tips on entering Honfleur. As the huge single gate opened we pulled in the ropes and were first to leave the lock. The sea was comfortable as we sailed out along the long line of markers that identify the channel into Ouistreham. Soon even the distinctive tall lighthouse had gone out of sight and we enjoyed a pleasant trip along the coast although we kept well off the shore to avoid the many shallows. Barry took the helm any time I wanted a break and it was great to have him there. Still, my Dad has been my first mate on this journey and he is missed.

Before long we picked up the markers that led into the Seine estuary. With Le Havre off to our left we lined up the markers and took up a line just north of the channel so as not to get in the way of any commercial traffic. Mar called us on the phone and I was relieved to hear that she had made it to Honfleur without incident. She was calling to say that three British naval boats had left Honfleur and we would pass them before long. Pretty soon the three boats came into view. They weren't ships, they were about fifty-footers and fast too. We exchanged waves, the type you make with your hand as well as the one that the boats cause.

The lock at the entrance to Honfleur opens on the hour and our timing was either very lucky or just spot-on, probably just lucky. This lock is unusual in that you tie onto floating bollards recessed into the lock side and held in place by a frame. These bollards float up and down with the water, so you don't have to do as much rope work you just have to watch in case a bollard gets stuck on its frame. We passed through the lock and found a good mooring on the quayside. Some of the other boats went past us and under the lifting bridge so they could enter the main or inner harbour where you pay premium mooring rates and you have to raft five boats deep. Honfleur is the most picturesque town we have seen on our travels. Trendy cafés line the harbour. This is where France's most beautiful people come to dine on seafood and fine wines. We found a café and the waiter found a table away from the beautiful people for us. We sat in our corner and drank the most expensive beer I have ever had. It tasted just the same as cheap beer.

The following morning I drove the car to a quiet car park where you could park free of charge. I tried to make the car look as inconspicuous as possible, then locked it up and returned to the boat.

The tide does funny things in the Seine estuary. It is possible to start at low water in Honfleur and then, with the tide pushing you, head up the river for the next 120 kilometres to Rouen, and have the tide push you all the way. We entered the lock along with several other boats, some of them wooden sailing boats on their way to the tall ships festival in Rouen. They weren't themselves tall ships, not yet at least but they will be one day. But the majority were fast expensive, plastic types, and they had boats to match too.

The gates opened and it was like the chequered flag being dropped at the Monaco Grand Prix. White Tupperware boats with petrol engines and menopausal skippers with white and navy caps gave it their all and left us in their wash. As they sped into the distance we crossed the shipping channel and once again took up a position just to the left of the markers. This kept us out of the way of those bigger boats who are earning a living.

The skyline here is dominated by the enormous *Pont De Normandie* suspension bridge. We timed the cars going over it and it took over three minutes on average, which is a long time if you, like me, don't like driving at an altitude normally occupied only by the international space station. The estuary is not very interesting. The sides are mostly concrete and you get the impression that nothing short of concrete would be able to cope with the strong currents and subsequent erosion.

It was at about this point that Mar realised that we were, strictly speaking at least, at sea. Mar doesn't like the sea, in fact she doesn't like water of any type but especially the sea. I explained that it would get narrower as we made more progress and that there was nothing to worry about. Mar started doing the washing up and any other cleaning she could find to help keep her mind off the sea. We passed a ship called the Wicklow Star and enthusiastically waved at another Irish vessel. No one waved back so we kept going.

Each marker on the estuary has its own number so we marked each one off on the chart as we passed it by. We passed the entrance to the Tancarville ship canal, which is an alternative route to Le Havre if you want to avoid the most exposed part of the estuary. We continued on past the small town of Vieux-Port which doesn't actually have any port.

The river had narrowed now and on the left hand bend here we are met with a frightening sight. A ship was coming for us at full speed. I swung to the right to get out of his way and it became clear he did not even see us. It was only as he passed us that he spotted us and immediately slowed down. It was too late for us though, his enormous wash was just in front of us and there was nothing for it but to point the boat into it. The water broke over the front deck before the nose pointed down into the trough then smashed into the next wave. I called into Mar to hold on as her newly washed delph went flying off the table and onto the floor. As the boat continued to pitch on the swells with a lessening Doppler effect, I give the controls to Barry and got inside to see how Mar was. She wasn't coping well. Mar doesn't like even small waves and ones that come in through the galley window without warning are especially unwelcome. There was talk of going home at the next port and "Why couldn't we have a mobile home in Wexford like everyone else in Dublin?"

Eventually we got closer to Rouen and, as we did, we noticed the smoke of a fire behind us. Strangely the smoke was catching up with us. Eventually it became clear that the smoke was not from a fire. It was from a big warship that was coming up behind us. It must be on the way to Rouen to make repairs, I thought. No engine should smoke that much. As it got closer we realised that it was a Russian Naval ship, complete with its own helicopter. As they passed us by we photographed them, they photographed us, we both waved, then their wash upset Mar and she started talking about the advantages of a caravan over a boat.

At about 1pm we passed Jumiéges. There is a ferry here and we gave way to it as it crossed to the other side. On the river went and the scenery got better, with chateaus looking down on us from steep tree-covered banks. Occasionally white rocky outcrops peppered the banks, making a patchwork effect with the trees.

It was 4pm when we arrived in Rouen and we moored up in the new *Port De Plaisance* in The *St Gervais* Basin. There were two boat rallies here, one was made up of inland waterways boats and the other was sea-going yachts. My loyalties were torn, but I was saved from making the call by the *Capitaine De Port* who arrived along in a rib to direct us into a mooring alongside the yachts. We had travelled one hundred-and-twenty kilometres since we left Honfleur at 9am that morning.

The port was at the seaward side of the town and all the tall ships were a little further upriver. After we tied up we introduced ourselves to our neighbours, who were delighted to meet more people with whom they could not converse. Then we went up town to see the tall ships. All along the quayside they had erected a tent village. Most of the tents were restaurants; it was chuck wagon heaven only on a more upmarket scale. You could buy a paper hat for five euro and, if you were willing to give up your first-born, you could buy a cup of tea. My sister decided to treat us to dinner in one of the tent restaurants which came complete with its own wooden floor and sexy young dancers too. In all the years that I've being pulling into the chuck wagon on the N1 I've never seen that.

Before we finished our main course a group of four actors came out, two male and two female. They were going around to each table in turn doing what I since discovered is called art in motion. Now if you don't understand art in motion, and I don't, it's best to take your lead from anyone who looks arty. I quickly spotted just such a man at the next table; he was wearing facial makeup, the type once made famous by Marcel Marceau, and he wore a black beret, but not the white gloves.

When he clapped, I clapped, when he laughed, I laughed, and when he stood and called "*encore encore*", so did I.
Barry got the bill and the waiter got his credit card. He has been leading a sedentary life since. That night there was a fireworks display. The French use more fireworks than the Chinese do. We returned to the boat for more wine and to allow our neighbours an opportunity to try out their one word of English and we replied with our French word. My sister Ann is a fluent French speaker so I try to keep her away from French people as much as I can. She was showing me up. It proved a bit difficult to isolate her because there are an awful lot of them

in France. I wondered where they all came from. Barry, like myself, is fluent only in English. Barry is also the best grubber on the planet. No matter what grub you put in front of Barry, he will eat it, and if there happens to be a drop of champagne around at the same time, that's all the better. He is a joy to have on a boat. He'd never show you up.

Sadly the time soon came for Ann and Barry to get their flight home. I was not sure how things would go without them. Mar had been afraid to go on deck since she realised that we were at sea, and she had been talking about going home to buy a caravan since the Russians bounced us around with their smokey ship.

Now I suddenly had no crew and would have to manage on my own, with Mar as just a passenger. It had been great to have Barry or Ann to jump off with a rope or even just to take the wheel to give me a break. Now it was all down to me. We waved goodbye as the boat slipped out into the strong current that is the Seine. We planned to press on for another forty kilometres inland before we would meet the first lock. As the lads waved goodbye I accelerated into the powerful current. Again I ticked each marker on the chart as we passed it. Mar wasn't enjoyed the trip since we left Ouistreham and I was keen to ensure that things went smoothly until she settled in.

The scenery had become bland again and our progress against the current grew slow. We passed under the bridge at *Oissel* but I couldn't stop or I wouldn't have got to the lock before it closed. We kept going, past *Elbeuf* and the scenery began improving again. Then eventually we rounded a gentle righthand bend and the lock was in front of us. We had to wait quite a while before the huge gates opened and the traffic lights showed a green light. Then we slowly entered the enormous lock. We could have done a figure of eight in it. I breathed a sigh of relief as we passed through this, our first lock on the river Seine. This was it. It was official: we were on an inland waterway again for the first time since the start of May. I felt Titanic, I felt Colossal. Passing through this lock signalled the completion of an enormous task - one that began in Limerick nine weeks previously. For Marion it was a milestone for different reasons: Mar had been looking forward to a quiet waterway and hopefully we had now found it.

"Will you take the back rope Marion?" I asked, as the sharp end of the boat was beginning to wander about a bit in the lock. "No…I'm not coming out of the cabin…I'm too nervous," came the reply. "I know I'm a burden to you Harry but I can't come out." I knew she was a burden too, so we laughed and the boat didn't wander about in the lock too much.

When the lock was full the lock keeper opened the upper gates from his special 'Control Room' at the top of a tower.
Just past the lock and in the fresh water of the non-tidal Seine we swung right and pulled into a quiet mooring beside a restaurant. It was nicely tucked in behind an island. Ours was the only boat there.
"Ah Monsieur, Bienvenu en France, Irlande Oui? I have a bateau also, you have bateau, I have bateau therefore we are ami. I have voiture, I can take you to wherever you like, mon bateau ese joli, your bateau ese joli too." We shook hands and it dawned on us both that I have no French, and so we had run out of common vocabulary, so our new friend drove off and we never saw him again.

Chapter Nine

Legless

W<small>E HEADED TO</small> the nearby restaurant. Here the gulls and gannets gave way to the swans and ducks once more. We chose to eat outside overlooking the river and the ducks. That way if we didn't like the food, the ducks would eat the evidence and the waiter would be none the wiser. I like ducks so I ordered one in an orange sauce.

A woman who was probably a little older than she would like to be has been unlucky in love and sits at the table beside us to lament the passing of a sweet relationship. Tears, sobbing and wine are never a good mix even though they go together so often. Eventually she interrupted us and, in perfect French, she told us all about her love life, or her lack of a love life, I'm not sure which. Luckily we have no French so we didn't understand any of what she told us and we didn't have to form any mental images. After talking to us for about twenty minutes she felt better, made her apologies and left. I don't think she ever realised that we didn't understand a word she said.

The ducks didn't have to partake in any cannibalism and went hungry as we ate a smashing meal and washed it down with some rosé wine, and then some more rosé wine, and I think there might have been another bit of rosé wine after that too.

The next morning we awoke to beautiful sunshine and scenery to match. We took the bikes and cycled the few hundred yards into Poses for a coffee, which we enjoyed at a table on the footpath outside a café. With no tides to worry about we could take our time and I felt Mar was getting a bit more relaxed now.

Later we untied and headed off along the river, past several large barges, some of them with their cars aboard and they were all loaded down to the waterline. Occasionally two of them were joined together, end to end. The one behind does the driving and they must be near on impossible to control.
Before long we arrived in Les Andelys. Here the countryside is dominated by the fantastic Chateau Gaillard, built by Richard the Lionheart in 1197 to prevent the French king from getting access to Rouen. We climbed the hill to the chateau on its summit. The views of the Seine valley in either direction make you feel like you are a bird in the sky. The scenery just goes as far as the eye can see in all directions.

We returned to the boat with sore legs and eyes to match. Hang on, we suddenly thought: the tide has gone out. It has well gone out, what has happened? The water has disappeared.

I stepped onto the floating jetty and it didn't rock any more, nor did my boat. The water in the river had dropped considerably since we went for our walk about three hours ago and now we can't move. Unperturbed I decided to have a siesta, confident that the water would return as mysteriously as it disappeared. When I awoke the water had not returned. I think it had dropped even further. "When will the water level come back up?" I asked a local who had a very shallow draft boat and was overly enthusiastically demonstrating its ability to motor in about two feet of water. My pidgin French just about got the message across. He raised his two arms up in a 'don't blame me' kind of way, and then made finger movements to indicate rain fall. It was apparent that we were in trouble.

Confirmation came from the local tourist information office, who kindly told us all about a boat that was stuck there for weeks, only a few seasons ago. "The harbour has silted up you know?" Well, I had come to realise that myself and thought that it might be a good idea if someone in the French Inland waterways authority, the VNF, might like to give it a mention at the next 'Where will we send the dredger to?' meeting or perhaps mention it on the charts. Still none of this was going to help us.

I thought of getting a winch and attaching it to the marker at the harbour entrance and dragging the boat out backwards. But the plan didn't seem very likely to meet with any great success. Given that the prospect was for our adventure to end here in Les Andelys I decided to have another look and do what ever could be done before the water dropped any further.

The ropes on the boat were as tight as banjo strings and if I untied them the boat might have fallen over to the far side. About four or five inches of hull, which would normally be beneath the water line, was now exposed. However, most of this was at the front of the boat, not the back where the propellers were.

The girl in the tourist office said that the harbour had silted up so that would imply that the bottom was soft mud and, indeed, a poke with the boat hook confirmed this.
I fired up the engines and gave it lots of power in reverse. Slowly we inched backwards towards the harbour entrance and the deep river. The engines suck in water from beneath the boat and use this water to cool themselves. But one of those inlets got blocked with thick mud. I could see the temperature gauge climbing, but as soon as I let off the revs we came to a sudden stop again. I knew I didn't have much time before the engine got too hot so I gave it all to get us out before it was too late. As we got closer to the entrance we got more water beneath us and soon we were afloat and drifting backwards into the river and into the path of a large barge.

I had to turn off the engine, which was now getting too hot, and just continue on one engine until I got a chance to clean the mud out of the filter.

About thirty minutes later we came to a lock. As with the first lock, they have constructed three locks of different sizes all beside each other. This is to accommodate boats of differing sizes. It's normal to give boats like ours the smallest one unless we are sharing the lock with a bigger vessel. Here we had the lock to ourselves and it gave me a chance to clean the mud out of the filter. With that job out of the way we had the use of both engines again. We continued on to *Ile Emient* where the chart said there was a mooring, but the man who wrote the chart had a tendency to tell little porkies. I was later told the chart wasn't wrong, it was just aspirational. I think VNF stands for "Visionary Not Functional."

We found a mooring at Vernon in The Vernon Yacht Club. It was nice to find a mooring that actually existed in real life and not just on the chart. The *Capitan* came down to our boat and introduced himself. He gave us loads of brochures and explained all of the local attractions.

Vernon was the site of some of the most fearsome fighting in the Second World War. I walked across the bridge over the river where there were a number of plaques:

> *In honoured reverence of all our comrades and*
> *of the townsfolk of Vernon, who gave their lives*
> *in the battle for the liberation of the town*
> *August 1944*
> *"They died so that we might live"*

Another plaque commemorates the brave fight fought by the men of :

> *The Nottinghamshire Sherwood Rangers*
> *Yeomanry Royal Armoured Corps.*

When you look from this spot across the river to the steep wooded banks on the opposite side where the German guns were dug in, it becomes apparent how difficult it must have been for those men to cross this river on rafts and make the advance.

While I was there I needed to pick up a piece for one of the exhausts that didn't survive the revving up necessary to get out of the harbour in Les Andelys. The folk in the chandlery, who didn't have any English between them, told me it will be the next day before they get the part in. That sounded fair enough to me and so we relaxed in Vernon.

There was a chateau beside the harbour that was hit during the war and the locals rebuilt the damaged tower. A bridge nearby that was missing a span stood as a reminder that this place was not always as peaceful as it is today. The main feature here is the mill house which stands on part of an even older bridge. It is a precarious-looking structure and it has been maintained by the locals of Vernon over the past few years.

When the part arrived I fitted it without any great problems and we were on our way again.

We left Vernon pretty much as we had found it and continued up the Seine. The Seine doesn't flow south, preferring to go east, then west then east again and then west again so that for every single mile south you travel you travel about thirty miles snaking east and west. They will probably straighten it some day. We needed to make good progress here to make up for the lost time. Anyway, I now had itchy feet, I wanted to keep going, I wanted to explore.

We came to Limay, another town with another remnant of a bridge, more evidence of how France suffered in the war. We spent the night on a jetty with no other boats for company. In the morning we passed under the lowest bridge we had come to so far, it links two Islands the *Ile Da Limay* and the

Ile L'Aumone. We had to drop the radar mast and the VHF antenna to squeeze under it.

I had noticed that a lot of people set up tents and all sorts of supplies to see them through long fishing trips and under the bridges appeared to be a favoured location. This bridge was an exception only because this family had brought everything you could imagine. Then, of course, the penny dropped: they have no fishing rods. To this family the bridge was their home. This was the face of homelessness in France.
The children waved enthusiastically at us as we passed, we waved back, but we were not sure what to do or say. In Ireland they live on roundabouts at busy motorway intersections, and here they live under the roads.

We continued heading south, with Limay fading into the distance behind us. I made a note on the chart just in case we ever passed this way again *"Low bridge."*

We cruised in warm summer sunshine. Jeans and jumpers gave way to shorts and T-shirts. This was French boating as you dreamt it should be. I still had to think twice about it, and I had a good look around me, to let it all sink in. Yes, we did make it to France, we were cruising on the French waterways, we did it, we really did cruise down the Atlantic south west coast of Ireland, we did cross the Celtic Sea, and the Channel too, and we really were here in the French inland waterways. I felt like a Master Mariner. I felt I had achieved something substantial in my life, something I would remember for ever. Now I was equipped with the story to bore the socks off my children, my grandchildren and my great grandchildren too.

We were at a lock; well we were waiting below the lock for the lock keeper to open the gates. There was nowhere to tie up. There was never anywhere to tie up, and still we waited. The lock keeper was probably trying to keep me in my place, let me know who is boss, but I felt unbeatable. I held the boat in mid-channel, motionless against the current and wind. Every time the bow moved an inch to the left or right I corrected it so that it stayed stationary. The waiting game continued. I could have learnt a foreign language in the time we had been waiting there. "Maybe he is waiting for a barge to come along?" says Marion, "No," I said, "there is nothing behind us." At the same time I looked over my shoulder to confirm what I had just said. "Oh my God!" A two-hundred foot Hotel Barge was sitting only a few feet away from me, also threading water. "You feckin eejet, you stupid feckin eejet. Why didn't you look behind you?" said Mar. Humbly, I moved *Driftwood* over to the right to let the colossal vessel pass. Then the gates opened, and the green light came on, and the hotel barge, '*The Renoir*' filled the huge lock but kindly the manufacturers had left just enough room to squeeze us in behind him.

It's a daunting experience to be raised up in a huge lock with an equally huge hotel barge. If he drifts left a bit or back a bit he will squash us flat. Worryingly, the barge doesn't use any ropes to hold stationary in the lock, the skipper preferring to demonstrate his skills by treading water. In an attempt to regain some of my pride I decided to do the same. We sat and waited again, and nothing happened. Occasionally there was French garble on the VHF radio. Still we waited, still nothing happened, then the lock keeper opened a window in his tower, stuck his head out, and roared at some idiot in the lock who was supposed to move his boat over to the left and had been told

repeatedly on the VHF to do so. I moved the boat over to the
left, the lock filled and we continued on our way but we kept
well clear of *The Renoir* hotel barge because there was nothing
I could do to regain any credibility now.

Conflans is the barge capital of France, or so the charts say, and
when we gently cruised into the town we could see why. They
were rafted together because there was not enough quay side
space. Some of them were moored five and six deep. On our left
hand side the River L'Oise {The French pronounce it Le Waz}
entered the river Seine. This is another beautiful river and we
felt we would love to go up it but we didn't have any charts of
it. There is a boat shop in Conflans so we found a spot to tie up
and I got my bike and went looking for the boat shop. It was
getting close to 5pm and I was still racing around on my bike
looking for the shop.

I had forgotten to bring my English/French dictionary
and that meant that I may as well have left my tongue behind.
Things were getting a little bit desperate now - I needed to
get the charts and time was running out. Then a police car
came around the corner so I put out my hand. The two police
officers speak perfect French, as you might expect, but not a
word of English. I managed to tell them that I was looking
for the boat shop and they tried to tell me where it was but I
could not understand them. Then, through hand signals and
so on, I realised that they were telling me to follow them. The
police car headed off and I pedalled as fast as I could behind. I
was laughing to myself at the same time: "I'm getting a police
escort in France." We continued for about a mile only to find
that the shop was closed. I thanked my two police men friends
and pedalled back to the boat.

"Will we try to go without any charts?" asked Mar. "Trouble is we don't even know how far it is to the next town," I said. Marion made us something to eat and we relaxed for a while. Then a boat came along. It was a catamaran and it was flying a red duster, but most importantly it turned and went up the L'Oise. Mar looked at me. "Will we follow them?" she asked. "You bet!" We revved it up and off we went.

As we followed the cat up the L'Oise, evening was closing in. On we went and when the navigation changed to the righthand bank, we followed the cat: when he went to the left bank we followed too, and when we came to a bridge we used the same arch. You are not supposed to navigate thirty minutes before sunset and I was concerned that we were getting close to that deadline. With no idea how far it was to the next mooring, the cat put on the power and pulled away, leaving us in the middle of nowhere with no idea where we were.

We continued on up the river past where they were building a lovely new harbour but you couldn't enter it because they hadn't finished building it yet and had put a chain across the entrance, no doubt because the first customer has to be the mayor or the president of France, or the General Secretary of the United Nations or just someone important.

Before much longer we came to a bridge and a town then, as if by magic, a marina opened up on our port side. We had reached Port Cergy. We went in slowly, which was just as well as this is the smallest, most compact marina I have ever been in. Added to that it is surrounded on two sides by Brasseries and on the other two by balconied apartments. Everyone was watching to see how many boats I would bump before I got tied up. At every table the guests put their knife and fork down beside their plates and then they sat back to watch a Paddy make a mess of mooring up. Now it's important to understand that, of all the skills a good skipper must have, the most trying and most difficult skill is to moor a boat when you have an audience. It is made all the more difficult when the mooring is as tight as they are in Port Cergy. I didn't think I would have enough room to turn around if I couldn't find a space. Luckily I didn't need to. A yachty indicated to a vacant mooring that was probably constructed with a canoe in mind.

The harbour is round in shape and the boats moor with the bow into the harbour wall where there is a small floating jetty. This is where it's nice to have twin engines. Moving at the same speed that fingernails grow at, I edged slowly into the gap. Fenders on both sides rubbed at the same time, but we were in and I felt I had done us proud. I expected a round of applause, but nothing happened, they just returned to their meals. I knocked off the engines and poured a Guinness!

Port Cergy reminds me of Honfleur. Both places are very similar except that Port Cergy is a very modern version and they don't rip you off here with the same blatancy that they do in Honfleur. I went to hook up to the mains electricity but those cunning French people, they have done it again. You need a special plug, a plug you can probably only get in Paris, and then only in the one shop and that probably will have closed early on the day you get there. One thing is for sure: I won't be able to get one from the *Capitan de Port* because this is Bastille weekend and no one works this close to the big holiday.

I considered firing up my noisy Lidl generator as payback but thought better of it. I could survive on battery power for a few days. Here Mar was at last at her ease. This was the France we had come looking for. It was beautiful, it was romantic, and it was a warm French evening, and so we went to one of the cafés overlooking the port and had a meal.

We should have stayed in Cergy for a second night, but now that we had found a peaceful waterway I wanted to see more, I was keen to see what's round the next bend in the river because around every bend there was a sight I had never seen before. It was all new, it was all an adventure.

In the hot sun of Bastille Day eve we continued on up the river. We passed the island of *Les Aubins* and the chart revealed that there was a small port tucked in behind it. The island is large and we couldn't see the mooring described in the charts. So we decided to take a look, but soon the depth sounder warned of impending trouble. We reversed back out and decided to go to Boran Sur Oise instead. There is a boat club there and a town with cafés and a shop too. When we arrived at the boat club it turned out that we were the only boat there and the town's folk had set up a marquee at the water's edge. A big celebration was planned for later that night with a band, BBQ and open air dancing. They had about two dozen tables set up, complete with tablecloths and candles. They had lights hanging from the overhanging trees and it all looked fabulous. We felt a bit like we were intruding, but there was nowhere else to go.

We needed to get some provisions so we wandered up the town, only to find that everywhere seemed closed until we spotted a solitary open shop. We picked up chops, burgers and other

BBQ bits and returned to the boat. That's when we realised that we couldn't really light a BBQ because it would look a bit awkward with the locals having their BBQ beside us. So we put the grub in the fridge and had a clear-out-the-larder meal - that's when you eat everything that is at, near, or just past, its 'Best Before' date.

We spent Bastille Day tied to the river bank just below Boran sur Oise. The barges weren't moving on account of the day it was, so we didn't have to worry about the boat getting bounced off the river bank. Boran sur Oise, like all French rural towns was sleepy, but this one was so sleepy that it was in danger of slipping into a fatal coma. We went for a cycle through the town and were surprised that no tumble weeds were blowing around the place. We found a self-service laundrette that was open so we decided to go back to the boat and return with our laundry.

After a while a man who looked like Eddie Murphy came in to do his laundry. He asked where we were from and when we said Ireland his face lit up with an expression that said: "Don't go anywhere. I'll be back in a minute," and he ran to the boot of his car. He returned, with a box and a look on his face that said 'you're going to love this.' We looked on, anxious to see what was in the box. He pulled over a chair so he would be comfortable, and he was anticipating this was going to take a while.

Eddie opened the box and said, "*chaussure por madam?*" "Shoes?..." I said. "You want to sell us bloody shoes?" Unperturbed Eddie held a tacky-looking high heel and stroked the finish, encouraging Marion to do the same but Mar had no interest. Next he produced a runner and held it in the same way, rambling on in French about its merits.

I fumbled with the English/French dictionary trying desperately to find *fuck off* but they didn't list it. Then Eddie accepted he was not going to flog any footwear but he was still in selling mode and produced some sunglasses that only Elton John would wear. Eventually he accepted that these two Irish knob jockeys are not the suckers he thought we were. He closed the box, took his chair and sat in the corner of the laundrette like a child in a huff.

When we returned to the boat I lit the BBQ and we relaxed and enjoyed the quiet. Soon you could hear the noise of a distant outboard engine. Sooner than I'd like it got a lot closer. Then a speedboat rounded the bend at a speed that would get a fully loaded Airbus A320 off the ground. "Jeaaasssus..." said the skipper. "Is that an Irish flag?" Pat as it turns out, is from Limerick and his partner Diane is Parisian. They tied alongside and we enjoyed an afternoon chatting in the sun. Pat gave me his charts because I had none and we used packets of Irish King Crisps and cans of Heineken as our currency.

The next day France returned to normal and we navigated up the river, eventually stopping in Compiegne, a large town that holds sad memories for French Jews. This is where many of them were held prior to being transported to the concentration camps during the Second World War.

There were a lot of sand barges around Compiegne. They move up and down the river. Sometimes two sand barges are stuck together stern to bow to make one very long sand barge. As they ply up and down, their wash puts quite a strain on the mooring ropes so I had to put out extra fenders and some more ropes. They seemed to be moving sand from A to B while others barges seemed to move it from B back to A. Apparently moving sand from one place to another is big business in France. In fact you would be forgiven for thinking it is the national sport. Maybe they were building a huge sand castle somewhere. Nobody seemed really sure what they do with all that sand.

Just above the town there was a small pleasure boat harbour but it was full when we arrived, so we returned to the main public jetty in the town centre. There was an English couple on a boat here, James and Helen, and we enjoyed each other's company for the afternoon. Then a knob from Belgium came along and spoiled it all. Not all Belgians are knobs. In fact it may be that this one had been gifted with all the knobism that normally would be shared among the population of any small country. He sat on our boat, invited his knob friends along, drank our wine and spoke only to his knob friends, but he did so in Flemish. Now like most people, Flemish is a language I am quite illiterate in. If it's OK to fight fire with more fire, then it's OK to fight bad manners with more bad manners. There is nothing wrong with being rude to rude people, they don't know any better, and don't take offence. So I uprooted the knob, sent him back to his own boat, and we went uptown for a pizza.

There is a fine ship's chandlery across the river and there is also a refuelling barge. We hadn't taken on any diesel since Honfleur so I filled up and took a wander around the chandlery too. All I bought was a sticker that listed all the national flags and told you what country they are from. I was surprised to see that so many had red, white and blue flags of one sort or another. I still have to refer to it regularly to identify which country some boats are from.

The next morning we headed upriver with James and Helen, as far as the junction with the river L'Aisne. They turned off here and we continued on as far as the canal at Longueil-Annel. Here, there were a lot of factories on the canal bank and there was a bit of a smell from them. It was probably some carcinogenic gas, but not the sort of thing you should get concerned about. Soon we were out into the countryside again and away from the risk of a slow tortuous death. The pace of life is much slower on the canals than it was on the river and Mar was having a ball.

Pont L'Eveque is a picturesque little village where the canal divides in two. The Canal De Nord is to the left but we kept right on the Canal de la Sambre a L'Oise, or just *de canal* to us. I was sorry I didn't overnight there because it was so pretty, but for some reason we just kept going.

Many of the locks in France are manned by young women, while at home the opposite is true. They are generally a very friendly and efficient bunch. At the lock in Pont L'Eveque the girl wished us a *Bon Journée* over the VHF. I decided that I had enough French by then to thank her and wish her well. Of course I was wrong. After my attempt I winked at Mar as if to say: 'Aren't I a smart boy?' But then the lockkeeper came back on the VHF and chattered to us non-stop for about three or four minutes. I hadn't a clue what she was talking about. So I turned to her so that she can see me, and I raised both hands in the air in a sort of 'I'm an imbecile who doesn't know French' kind of way. She got the message and we headed off and I made a mental note never to do that again.

The chart said that there is a marina in Chauny and this time the VNF have aspired to their aspiration. Ron and Pat are an English couple who run things around here. Ron is ex RAF and reminds you of the fact quite regularly, just in case you're the forgetful type. He retired recently but he admits that he has being saying that for the past twenty-two years. Ron took our ropes for us and helped us get sorted with electricity and water. It was great to meet English-speaking people and so we asked them to join us for a BBQ later. "Ah, so that was you on the VHF earlier," said Ron. "I was listening to it in Philippe's boat," he said. "The lockkeeper was trying to tell you that the canal is closed at St Quentin for about four days." "Oh," I said, "I had no idea what she was saying, it must be great to be able to speak French?" I said. "I don't know," said Ron, "I am here for the past three years and I only know about three words. It was Philippe who translated for me."

The BBQ went on until the early hours.

Chapter Ten

Vive La Difference

ANN AND DES are coming over tomorrow to spend a weekend with us and they will have their two children, Conor, aged eight, and Sarah, aged twelve, with them. We were really looking forward to seeing them and having a bit of craic. I hired a car to collect them from Beauvais Airport and headed off with a map and a bottle of water. Three hours, one bottle of water, and several provinces later I arrived at Beauvais Airport. This is not a real airport at all, it's more an airfield with a cheap café stuck onto the side of it that charges expensive prices.

There was the usual slapping of backs when we all met up. Ann, who had just set a new 'excess baggage record' with Ryanair, loaded the cases, bags and holdalls into the boot. What she could not fit into the boot she piled on top of Sarah and Conor. "Do many people speak French over here?" asked Ann. "Well it's the national language of France," I said. "That's nothing," said Des, "Wait till she has had a few drinks, we'll get no sense out of her. Annisms I call them." "I meant to say English, do many people speak English?" said Ann. "You can't redeem yourself now Ann," I said, as I missed my turn-off at the roundabout and had to go round again. "We're getting dizzy back here," says Conor. "I need to go to the toilet," said Sarah.

Three long hours later and we were back at the boat. Ron and Pat joined us again and the six of us had a fabulous evening. I remember Ann asking Ron why the English invaded France "We didn't," said Ron, "That was the Germans." "But the English invaded France too," said Ann. "No, we liberated France," Ron said. "I was in the RAF you know." "Do you mean like the Americans liberated Iraq?" asked Ann. "No," Said Ron, "We really were liberators."

Next morning Des and myself drove in the hire car back to Honfleur to collect my car, wondering if it is still in the car park where I left it three weeks earlier. We underestimated the journey. It took us five hours of motorway driving each way. Just as we were approaching Honfleur Des said: "Wow, will you look at that bridge." I don't love heights that much and the *Pont De Normandie* suspension bridge is not my favourite place. I'd prefer to be in a dentist's chair. Up we went…and up further…and further. The space shuttle passed beneath us as it orbited the earth. I focused on the registration plate of the car in front. I didn't look left or right. If the car in front went over the side then I would blindly follow. Next thing I passed a guy on a bicycle: What the hell was he doing up there? He must have had a death wish. When we got across to the other side you could see the prints of my hands in the steering wheel. A week later you could still see them.

We arrived in Honfleur and it was still as cosmopolitan as I had remembered it. What's more, my car was still where I had left it, and it started first time. Not bad seeing as its ten years old, with a milometer that reads like a chassis number.

We got back on the road straight away. The journey had taken us much longer than we had expected, so we decided that we would stop at a motorway service area on the way back for a coffee. Then we missed the turn-off for the motorway service area so we had to make do with a coffee at a garage a few hours later. Next we missed another turn-off, followed by three more. Then the motorway maintenance people gave us directions which we didn't understand and it was by pure chance that we stumbled on Chauny again. Tired and hungry and with sore eyes, we pulled the cork from a bottle of Bordeaux and sat down with our feet up.

On the Sunday we came to a place called Pinon. There isn't much in Pinon, which is probably what makes it so attractive. It does have a picnic table on the canal bank and we made good use of it. Des made a Beef *Bourguignonne* as soon as we moored up. He is an excellent cook and it took quite a few bottles of wine to wash down all the beef.

The following morning I awoke early. The system we had devised was that whoever got up first had a few things to do. The first was to take the butter out of the fridge so it would be soft for breakfast. Then go to the boulangerie and buy a selection of breads and pastries. As soon as you returned to the boat it was time to put on the kettle and call the crew with a pot of tea at the ready.

The boulangerie is the meeting place in any French town and the centre of all gossip. Boulangeries don't just sell bread; they also sell some of the prettiest cakes and treats you are ever likely to come across. Every town has at least one boulangerie, as well as a café that will close for lunch, and a chemist. They must have a chemist because all French men have sclerosis of the liver and they need a constant supply of medication which they wash down with red wine. Don't get me wrong: the French, unlike 'Paddy De Pig' don't go to the pub in the evening and skull a dozen pints then arrive home to their wives pissed as a newt. The French, being more refined, choose to start sipping wine early in the day, but they never get drunk. They prefer to simply spend their lives in a constant state of tranquil intoxication.

The boulangerie in Pinon was in the local supermarket, which is right beside the canal. And this supermarket sold bottles of chilled champagne, even in the morning. Well, I thought, why not? When I got back to the boat I set the table and gave them all a shout. "Who wants champagne for breakfast?" I called out. "Oh sure I will so," said Ann without even the slightest hint of hesitation. It's the sort of thing I would never normally do, but I said: "What the heck, we'll be dead for a long time," and I popped the cork and so started another great day.

French men have it made. At one of the locks we passed through that day, we exchanged pleasantries with a sixty-something-year-old Frenchman who was leaning against his fence, while behind him his wife was in a pair of wellies digging quite a sizeable vegetable plot. Obviously he felt more at home at a supervisory level.

We bade him farewell and continued on to the next town.

In Bourg Et Comin it was my turn to cook. Now it has to be said that I am just not cut out to be a cook, but I'll have a go, which is probably the worst combination you can get. The rules that Des had laid down were that you could not use anything out of a packet. You could, however, use the extensive cookbook we had onboard. I decided to make fillet steak with Béarnaise sauce. I set the bar a bit too high there. I should have gone for a more minimalist approach and tried something like beans on toast. To be fair to my patrons, they ate everything, well, except for the Béarnaise sauce, but sure you couldn't blame them for that - it tasted like vinegar.

I woke the next morning to the sound of Des licking the boat. "What you doing Des?" I asked. "Ah you can still taste salt off her. You want to give her a good wash or she will rust away to nothing." So we started the day by soaping her down, and then we hosed her down. Des did his lick test again and this time he announced that she tasted positively bland. Just the way a boat should taste.

There were a few barges tied up in Bourg Et Comin also. Each of them were about two hundred feet long and one was getting a bit of work done to her in preparation for a new coat of paint. The skipper was taking advantage of the shade provided by a sycamore tree and enjoying a few cold beers with some other barge men. His wife, on the other hand, was busy with an orbital sander and it looked as though she had quite a bit of barge left to sand. I'm sure that if we had asked him nicely he would have told his wife to wash our boat too.

Des and myself mused about having our lives over again and how we would marry a French girl and buy her power tools on her birthday. Just then the husband said something to his wife and she put the sander down immediately and retired into the barge. It was a hot day and you could not stay out in the heat for too long. A short time later she emerged again with three cold beers for hubby and his pals, who are obviously incapable of any movement below the waist. Then she got back to the sanding. "Can you have two wives in France?" Des asked. "You could get twice as much work done if you had two of them."

We moved in the heat of the day to the next town on the chart, a small place called Berry au Bac. They said that there was a shop here but it's not true. There is a shop four miles from here. We tied up to the canal bank and considered having a BBQ. Trouble was we needed to get to a shop first. Now if we had a French wife there would have been no discussion about who was doing the cycling to the shop and who was going to wait in the local café drinking cold beer. But things were different on our boat and neither myself nor Des fancied our chances fighting with the women. So we walked them to the café, asked the girl behind the counter for directions to the shop, and left them to it.

It was a very hot day now and there is no shade to be had when you're cycling. We dodged trucks on the main road from Berry au Bac to somewhere equally quaint, and successfully made it to the turn-off.
Here we were cycling through cornfields on a minor road with no traffic on it. That's just as well because July is the cyclist season and anyone on a bike is fair game, unless of course it's a mating couple. Sure you have to let them breed in order to

keep the stocks up. Cars and trucks will risk hitting telegraph poles, fences, and even a head on collisions in order to run down a good cyclist.

We made it to the shop, which turned out to be a supermarket or *supermarché* as they say in France. We loaded up our backpacks with all sorts of goodies for the BBQ and some wine too. The man serving at the butchers counter looked at us with a look that said: 'Bet they're a gay couple.' Des picked up on this straight away and tried desperately not to look like my bitch. But it was too late and the more he tried to look macho, the more camp he appeared. When we had finished our shopping I suggested we leave before the butcher asked Des for a kiss.

Out of the air conditioned supermarket, and into the hot stuffy air. We were not exactly *Tour De France* material and our legs were feeling it now. The journey back to the boat seemed to take forever. When we finally arrived back the women were nowhere to be seen. We loaded the fridge with the grub and headed back to the café. True to form, there they were, sitting behind a few empty Heineken bottles. *"Deux biére grand s'il vous plaît"* I called to the girl, who had lied to us when she said it was only four miles to the shop, more like twenty-four I thought. Or was that just me getting older? I felt it was my duty to visit neighbourhood hostelries, and sample the local beverages. It's not easy, you know.

There was a woman in the corner who had a poodle with her. Now, the poodle is the dog favoured by childless couples. This is because poodles enjoy being treated like humans, and there is evidence that this one has recently had a visit to the grooming parlour, where she enjoyed a cut, wash and blow-dry, with some ribbons to accessorise. "Fifi," as 'mummy' kept calling her, was dressed in a light green jacket thingy with a designer label on it. She was better dressed than most of the people in the café.

Fifi couldn't speak, at least not yet, but mummy kept talking to her, all lovey-dovey, anyway. There was an unhealthy amount of cuddling between mummy and Fifi and you felt that a long, wet, and explorative kiss was not far off. It was enough to make you throw up. Fifi must have sensed it too, and jumped to the floor to escape. But then Fifi let mummy down with a bang. It became apparent that no one had ever bothered to toilet train her, and she dumped in the middle of the floor. Mummy pretended not to notice, but to be honest it's hard to not see it. Stevie Wonder could see it. It was like we were drinking in a big kennel.

It appeared that the day had been rescued by the girl behind the bar who came out, picked up the dog mess with her hand, and put it in a bin. Yes, I did say, "with her hand." But guess what? She didn't wash her hands afterwards. I'm serious: she just continued on behind the bar. People were unaware and let her pour coffee and drinks for them. That's it, we were out of there, quick... before Fifi pisses all over us.

The following day we had to go through the *Sauterne de Bray*, a tunnel that takes about twenty minutes to get through. There are no tunnels on any navigable Irish waterway so we were a bit apprehensive. Traffic in the tunnel is by way of a one-way system. It is controlled by traffic lights, and an intercom to a control centre hidden in a secret location. The traffic light was red when we arrived, as of course it would be, so we tied up and waited. After waiting a while I got my well-thumbed English/French dictionary, a note pad with a few notes on it, and took on the dreaded intercom. The voice that came out of the little square box waxed lyrical about I know not what. The waiting continued and the light remained red. I took a camera and Sarah and myself photographed butterflies and the wild flowers that decorated the otherwise overgrown mooring. We surprised ourselves with the results, and we bored everyone else with them.

Then the silence was interrupted by a subterranean rumble. It wasn't an earthquake. A peek into the mouth of the tunnel revealed a large barge heading our way. It seemed to take the barge forever, and we watched with camera at the ready to capture the moment the barge emerged, and would be framed by the tunnel. When it did emerge it was a great sight, and to top it all they had their car on the back deck too. We exchanged salutes, and then Conor announced that the light had turned green. Those people in the secret control room must be watching everything.

In the tunnel Sarah used a bright torch to antagonise the many bats that were enjoying their sleep while hanging from the roof.
The tunnel is illuminated by lighting along its full length. About twenty minutes later we emerged out the other end. There, on the canal bank, was the control room. It didn't look as intimidating as I had imagined.

Reims is probably the largest town in this region; it vies with Epernay to be the centre of the Champagne area. The mooring in Reims is thoughtfully under a flyover in the city centre so you can expect to experience a spell of sleep deprivation. The heat was stifling, and it was Conor who had the idea of using buckets of cold water to soak our feet in. Conor is a quiet lad, but when he speaks you would do well to listen up. His bucket idea was a big hit, and it was used daily for the rest of the trip.

Still, Marion and myself had to walk back along the canal to the Lidl we passed on the way in. We wanted to buy a parasol to stop us getting burnt, but we must have lost track of distance, and it seemed that Lidl was much further away than we had thought. It was only because we had walked so far that we justified continuing on. Eventually we rounded a bend and there it was. We were the only customers there and they had enough parasols to keep most of France in the shade. I picked one up and Mar asked the assistant if there was any chance he could call a taxi for us. "No." came the response, nothing else just 'No.' Thinking that maybe he had misunderstood her, Mar phrased the question again, and got the same monosyllable response. "What part of Germany are you from?" I asked. I know how to get right under a Frenchman's skin when I have to. But he wouldn't rise to the bait. We walked all the way back to the boat carrying the parasol and dreaming of a cold beer.

Reims is famous for its cathedral and so it should be. Now don't get me wrong. I'm not the sort who waxes on about churches and the like. But in the case of *Notre-Dame de Reims* I'll make an exception. The kings of France were once crowned there and the magnificence of the building and its statues cannot be over emphasised. This thirteenth century church has survived many wars and not always without incident. There has been a place of worship on this site since before 496 AD when Clovis was baptised here by St Remi, the then Bishop of Reims.

We found a branch of McDonalds that dated from a more recent period, and we tucked into the first fast food we have had since coming to France. Fast food is not as popular here;

the French are much too proud of their culinary history to surrender to such gastronomic vulgarity.

Everything to do with Reims revolves around the cathedral or champagne, or both. On our way back to the boat we passed a couple sitting in a doorway. They looked to be homeless, and while at home in Dublin you might expect them to be knocking back bottles of Buckfast wine, not so in Reims. I'm not joking when I tell you that this pair were drinking champagne from a bottle by the neck. What a classy city. This is the benchmark against which I will measure all French towns from now on. They are such a sophisticated bunch, those French, you just have to love em. I wanted to take a photograph but Mar was pulling at my clothing to keep me moving. She has so much more tact than I do.

The following day Des, Ann and the kids had to head away to meet friends in the south of France but they planned to join us again before the end of the trip. The boat seemed very quiet without them, but after spending two nights in Reims I was keen to get to a peaceful mooring where the noise of traffic wouldn't disturb my sleep.

The French have a passion for making noise. French children learn from a very young age that by removing the baffle from an exhaust pipe, even the smallest moped can cause noise-induced hearing loss in your family, friends, and neighbours. This is a subject in most French kindergartens, and it is one that the French males take to easily, as all French males have inherited the noisy chromosome. Making noise is considered a measure of your maleness. The more noise you can make the more testosterone it is assumed you have flowing around in your system. Therefore, a noisy moped can make you a very suitable and sought after mate.

The noise does not just apply to mopeds. Most French conversations can be heard miles off, and it applies to bells too. In France everybody wakes up each morning to the sound of bells. Even if you moor miles from a town, on a canal bank in the middle of nowhere, someone will arrive along with a bell and ring it at 8am.

We left Reims behind us and sailed away through the many locks that only work some of the time. When they don't work you have to call the VNF on the intercom with your phrase book and an English/French dictionary at hand, and do your best. Some of the time they could understand me, but I never understood them. They are quite efficient and usually they arrive out to you in a matter of minutes. They open a big control box, look into it, curse a bit, throw a dirty look or two at the unresponsive gates and, if that doesn't work, then finally they give the control box a slap on the side and usually everything comes to life again.

Eventually the city surrendered and the countryside took over once more. We sailed along the narrow canal, occasionally meeting a barge. We passed a young couple on the canal bank who were obviously deeply in love. But you see, the French have impeccable manners, so they stopped, stood up, smiled and waved. Well, we waved back, as etiquette dictates you should do in such circumstances. Then we carried on, and so did they.

The day was extremely hot and we had no beer on board. We stopped on the canal bank and took the bicycles over a bridge in search of a cold drink. It wasn't long before we found a hotel, which is more than I can say for the young couple, and soon we were sitting in front of two cold Carlsbergs. It reminded me of that famous scene at the end of the film 'Ice

Cold in Alex.' We slept well on a good mooring on the canal bank undisturbed, although the following morning, at about 8am, I'm sure I could hear bells ringing.

Later we continued on through the *Souterrain du Mount-de-Billy*. This is a tunnel just under two-and-a-half kilometres long. There is a one-way traffic system and again it is controlled by traffic lights. The tunnels don't pose any problems themselves but it would not be the ideal place to start frying chips in the galley. It took about twenty minutes before we emerged out the other side and it is just like coming out of the cinema after the Sunday matinee on a sunny day.

We were heading to *Sillery* because everyone says you must see it. When we got there everyone else was there too, and there were no mooring places available, so we pressed on and promised to make time to visit some other time. We passed through another few locks, each one dropping us down closer to the level of the Marne river. At the lock at Conde Sur Marne there is a small diesel locomotive on the bank. It doesn't drive any more, but it once ran along tracks on the canal bank towing the barges. Now it acts as a flowerpot to please locals and tourists alike. A very humble end for a working engine.

There is a small marina here and we tied up for the night. Gerard was the *Capitan de Port* or, as he preferred to be called, *Gerard Bateau*. There are two cafés in Conde sur Marne and we tried both of them. The one nearest the marina does a supersized *biére* which gets it huge brownie points as far as I am concerned. Large beers are as rare as hen's teeth in this land.

There is a Champagne house in the village too, and Monsieur N.Potié does a mean bubbly. I have worked diligently acquiring a taste for the stuff. This could well be the start of a problem, but it's a lovely tasty problem.

Helen and James, the English couple we met in Compiegne, arrived into the marina and Helen asked us to join them on their boat. I grabbed a bottle of wine and headed over, eager for the sound of perfectly spoken English.

James is an electronic something-or-other and he had built his own electric fly-killing machine. It was like the ones you see in butchers' shops, except that James's ran off an ordinary car battery and it didn't kill any flies. The neon light, however, was excellent at attracting them and it looked like every fly in Conde sur Marne was now happily enjoying a broken fly-killing machine on James's boat, and eating me at the same time. But James was not the sort to admit defeat too quickly and kept fiddling with the failed killing machine. Now the flies had grown large and healthy, mainly on a diet of my flesh washed down with a nice Bordeaux. But then there was a crackling sound, or to be precise the sound of flies being fried in James's machine. James had located the fault and fixed it. The device was kept busy for quite a while catching up with the backlog.

When we returned to the boat I checked my phone and there was a text message on it from my sister Ann and her partner Barry. They had sourced cheap flights and would meet up with us in Epernay for our last night in France.

There is a canal junction at Conde sur Marne, and we decided to head along the canal that will eventually join the river Marne. The weather was still fantastic and we bade farewell to

Gerard Bateau, as well as James and Helen and continued on our journey.

Later we came to a mooring at the foot of the champagne vineyards. This was *Mareuil sur Ay* with its fine pontoon moorings. The canal widened here and there were showers and toilets at the *Capitan de Port's* office. It seemed that everyone there is employed one way or another in the champagne business and every home was selling the stuff at a fraction of Dublin prices. The more we drank the more we saved. I was hoping to save enough to buy a new boat.

We went up the town for a meal out. The café at the square serves Guinness but I avoided it. Stout seldom travels well and, unless there is a good turnover of Guinness, you could well end up with the stout-two-step, and then it would be a while before you could wander too far from a loo. The two-step has left its mark on many a man, as well as his underwear, over the years.

We enjoyed a fine meal and a bottle of wine, then every business in the town closed. This is normal in rural France. Nightlife is a concept that never really caught on here. They are just far too romantic to go out at night. French people prefer to stay at home with the shutters tightly closed and make more French people.

It was August now, which is the holiday season. You would imagine that this would be a very busy period for the cafés, restaurants, and hotels and it would be if they didn't close down for two weeks to head away on their own holiday. That's what I like about France; in other nations it's the government that runs the country, but here the people call the shots, not the government.

In the morning there were people swimming in the canal, although I could not help feeling that they were not so much swimming as just 'going through the motions.' I'd love to have got in for a dip too but my Hepatitis-B vaccination wasn't up to date.

We needed to return to Conde sur Marne, and to Gerard Bateau. Des and Ann were going to meet us there, so in the midday heat we wandered back up the river and through the few locks. My phone rang just as we reached the first lock. "Hi Harry, we will be there soon, we're just forty kilometres from Conde sur Marne now." Ann was excited and couldn't wait to get back to the boat. "You must have left early this morning," I said. "We were on the road at eight, and it's 3pm now, that's seven hours driving." "I'll have a cold beer ready for you, see you soon."

When we pulled into the marina at Conde, we were surprised to see that they weren't there before us. An hour went by, and still no word. I was getting worried, so I rang them. "We missed the turn off on the motorway," said Ann. "Where are you now?" I asked. "Where are we now Des?" asked Ann. "We are on a motorway….somewhere….we don't have a proper map so we're not sure where we are," said Ann. The conversation continued in a similar vein, and it was apparent that they were hopelessly lost. I got out my road map of France and we were able to identify the motorway they were on. A short time later we discovered that they were heading in the wrong direction. A long time after that, they managed to find a flyover and head back in the right direction.

It was 7pm when Des and Ann finally arrived at the boat, eleven hours after they had started what should have been a seven-hour trip. "Are you guys still talking to each other?" I asked. "Ah we are," said Ann. We opened a cold bottle of champagne and reminisced about events during the few days they were away, and all the bits of France that Des saw, but would have preferred not to have seen.

The next day Des and Ann were flying home so we drove to Epernay in the car first to do some shopping. Wine is considerably cheaper in France than it is in Ireland, so is everything else in France. Ann has no concept of a weight limit. Military refuelling aircraft have taken off with less liquid cargo than Ryanair was going to have to carry. Eventually she agreed to leave most of it in the car and we promised to bring it back home with us when we returned.

That afternoon we drove Ann, Des, Sarah and Conor to the train station in Epernay to catch the train to Beauvais. There we said our farewells. As the train pulled out Ann's head appeared out the window "Promise you won't drink our wine." "I promise I won't drink it Ann," I said.

We pressed on, getting closer and closer to the river Marne. The weather was just fantastic and children were jumping off the bridges into the water below. When you passed them by they tried to get themselves entangled in the propellers by swimming out from the banks as close to the boat as they could. I perfected the art of slipping into neutral just before I got too near, and the momentum carried us past them, where I could put her back in gear again.

All the way along we could see vineyards along the canal bank. It was a wonderful sight. Then we approached the last lock on The Canal Latéral á la Marne and it was a poignant moment. We entered the lock and the gates close behind us. Then slowly the water level dropped down, and when it stopped the gates in front of us opened and the mighty River Marne looked in at us. She was beckoning us to join her, so I put *Driftwood* into gear and we slid out of the lock onto the final silver pathway.

We turned left and went against the gentle current as we advanced towards the town of Epernay.

The Castellane Champagne house has a tower that is sixty six metres high and it dominates this part of the Marne valley. There is a boat club near the champagne house and we moored there beneath the shadow of the Castellane tower.

The *Capitan de port* took our ropes, and then he brought us to his office for the customary form filling. We filled out twenty-five forms, maybe even more; some of them were in triplicate. There were white forms, pink forms, and green forms; they asked every question you can think of, as well as a few you would never think of. Then he explained the workings of the washing machine and the showers, then the procedure to be followed if you required diesel and how to order a pizza. He gave us a package of brochures which included a coupon for a free tour of the Castellane Champagne Cellar. He invited us to have a drink in the club bar later that evening.

Mar and myself then got our bikes out and cycled the short distance to the train station to meet Ann and Barry. Before we got there we met them on the roadway. Hugs and handshakes were exchanged and we returned to the boat.

    Later we headed to the club bar. We could see that there was a large group of boaters there already. "What will we drink?" asked Marion. "Just see what everyone else is drinking," said

Ann. Everyone else was drinking champagne. The crowd were very welcoming; it was like the UN General Assembly. There were boaters from Germany, Britain, Netherlands, New Zealand, Belgium, France, as well as some more that I can't remember. I blame the champagne.

The atmosphere was great, each nation ribbing the next. "Do all you Irish reject the Lisbon Treaty?" "You Irish are not real Europeans you know!" "Your boat, is it Dutch?" "Yes," I said. "We sailed it here from Ireland." "You sailed in the sea in that little boat? See, in the Netherlands we build the best boats." The banter continued unabated, and Ann, Barry, Mar and myself opened another bottle of champagne.

"Why a turkey? You sent a turkey, why?" "Yes" agreed the German contingent, "We don't understand this whole turkey thing." There is no coming back from the turkey. Dustin was the nail in our coffin. "Johnny Logan was very good. You should have sent him." "Yes"… "Oh Yes" everyone agreed that Johnny was definitely a much better bet then the turkey.

I had a leg of lamb. Des had shown me just how to cook it to perfection. I'd taken it off the bone and now it was in the oven. Previously I had marinated it in olive oil, pesto, garlic and anything else that looked to be on the way out. Now it was time to get the BBQ on the way. I took the lamb out of the oven to rest a while and then, when everything was ready, I put it on the BBQ. The UN Assembly all wanted a bit. The aroma of barbecued lamb is up there with the best of them. It would tempt the statue of a saint down off his pedestal. We ordered yet more champagne and sat down for a scrumptious alfresco meal. The UN ordered pizza from the *Capitan*.

The festivities went on for several more bottles of champagne and always the atmosphere was one of friendly rivalry.

This was our last night in France, and I had imagined a civic ceremony with bands playing and fireworks, speeches by the Lord Mayor, and maybe Celine Dion would show up and sing something smooth and sexy to mark our departure. But in the end it wasn't like that, it was, all the same, a fantastic night, with great company, tinged, as it was, with a slight feeling of melancholy.

In the morning we packed the car, and said our farewells to the UN Assembly.

I turned the key to lock the door of the boat for the last time. Then we climbed into my car. Sitting there we felt really down. I started the engine, and we pulled out of the marina. As we did I saw the reflection of *Driftwood* in the mirror.

Things You should never say on a boat:

At least the engines are running fine.

The wind will probably drop at dusk.

This will be a handy spin across the pond.

These are perfect cruising conditions.

There is no way that we will hit that big ship.

French food is always good.

There's no problem - it's an offshore wind.

I don't think the waves on the Atlantic coast will be that big.

French wine never makes you sick.

www.driftwood.tv

A few details:

The trip was a total of 1,276 nautical miles from our mooring at Albert Marina on the northern end of the River Shannon to our current mooring on the River Marne. That's a little less than 1,500 statute miles.

The journey from Limerick to the French canals took about seven weeks, which included three weeks in Cornwall where we were stuck with bad weather and engine trouble.

The weather was always our biggest factor and it dictated our progress at sea. Sometimes waiting on good weather tested our patients.

The trip was one of the best experiences in my life. I don't think it will be my last.
If you find yourself with nothing better to do you could take a look at my website www.driftwood.tv where I have photos and some video clips of the trip too, enjoy.

Fair Winds
Harry.

References:

During the voyage we used the following books and charts:

Books:
Sailing Directions South & West Coasts of Ireland Written by The
Irish Cruising Club, eleventh edition 2006 published by Irish
Cruising Club Publications Ltd. ISBN No
0 9501717 9 4 and 978 0 9501717 9 1
This is an invaluable reference for anyone navigating this stretch
of waterway.

The Shell Channel Pilot 2006, by Tom Cunliffe. Published by
Imray Laurie Norie & Wilson. ISBN No: 0 85288 894 5.
This guide covers both the English and French coasts and is a
priceless navigation aid.

Reeds Nautical Almanac 2008.

Admiralty Leisure Folios:
SC 5622 Ireland - South Coast 1st Edition.
SC 5623 Ireland – South West Coast 1st Edition.
SC 5602 The West Country 8th Edition.
SC 5601 East Devon and Dorset Coast 7th Edition.

Admiralty Leisure Chart SC 1123 Western approaches to St George's Channel and Bristol Channel.

Imray Charts:
Imray C12 Eastern English Channel.
Imray C55 Dingle Bay to Galway Bay.
Imray C6 Salcombe to Lizard Point.
Imray C5 Bill of Portland to Salcombe Harbour.
Imray C7 Falmouth to Isles of Scilly and Newquay.

Admiralty Charts:
2495 Kenmare River
2125 Valentia Island
1819 Approaches to The River Shannon
2254 Valentia Island to River Shannon
2739 Brandon and Tralee Bays
2789 Dingle Bay and Smerwick Harbour
1540 River Shannon - Shannon Airport to Limerick.
1548 River Shannon – Ardmore Point to Rinealon Point.
1549 River Shannon – Rinealon Point to Shannon Airport.
1547 River Shannon – Kilcredaun Point to Ardmore Point.
2454 Start Point to The Needles
2613 France North Coast Cap De La Hague to Fecamp.
2345 Plans in South-West Cornwall
442 Lizard Point to Berry Head

Navicarte #1
La Seine aval du Harve á Paris

Carto-Guide Fluvial # 4
Île De France Champagne Ardennes Picardie.

Lightning Source UK Ltd.
Milton Keynes UK
UKHW022123101121
393751UK00010B/2456